300 FINANCE & ACCOUNTING QUESTIONS

That Every Finance Student & Professional Should Try!

By

Benjamin Bennett Alexander

© Copyright (2021) by (Benjamin Bennett Alexander) - All rights reserved.

It is not legal to reproduce, duplicate, or transmit any part of this document in either electronic means or printed format. Recording of this publication is strictly prohibited.

Every effort has been made in the preparation of this book to ensure the accuracy of the information presented. However, we do not warrant or represent its completeness or accuracy.

Dedication

To You The Reader, The World Is Yours

Knowledge is not what you can remember, but what you cannot forget"
Anonymous

"We are what we repeatedly do. Excellence, then, is not an act but a habit"
Aristotle

Feedback

Please let me know your thoughts about the book. I'm very interested to hear from you. Let me know how the book has helped you, and if you have any suggestions or questions please feel free to share them with me.

You can reach me at: benjaminbennettalexander@gmail.com

Table of Contents

Dedication iii
Feedback iv
Table of Contents v
Introduction vii
Present Value Table ix
1 Business Types & Corporate Governance 3
2 The Accounting Equation 6
3 The Income Statement 9
4 Balance Sheet & Double Entry Accounting 16
5 The Cash Flow Statement 25
6 Depreciation and Amortization 29
7 Leases 32
8 Revenue 36
9 Working Capital Management 38
10 Mergers, Acquisitions, & Reorganization 43
11 Equity and Dividend Policy 51
12 Performance Evaluation 59
13 Risk Management and Debt Capital 66
15 Investment Appraisal 76
16 Answers 80
17 Glossary 130
About Author 150

Introduction

Whether you an accountant, a finance and accounting student, a bookkeeper, an aspiring bookkeeper, or a non-finance person who is interested in finance –This book is for you. In this book, you will find **300 exam-type multiple-choice questions** that tackle some of the most important topics in accounting and finance. **Answers** and detailed explanations are provided at the end. Learning through tackling questions helps to build critical-thinking skills, improves comprehension and knowledge retention. So, what are we going to explore?

- We are going to start from the basics. We are going to explore the types of businesses that an individual and groups of individuals can set up, and the cons and pros of each type. We will also tackle the cornerstone of accounting – **the accounting equation and double-entry accounting.**

- We are going to explore the three most important financial statements in finance and accounting – **the income statement**, **the balance sheet**, and **the cash flow statement**, starting with the basics.

- We are going to tackle some of the most important elements of the balance sheet and the income statement – **revenue**, depreciation, amortization, **leases**, **deferred expenses**, prepaid expenses, and more.

- The fuel of any organization is **working capital**. Every finance person should be able to understand the mechanics of working capital management. We will explore some of the important ratios, methods, and techniques that accountants use to manage the working capital of organizations.

- We will not shy away from the accounting standards of **IFRS** and **GAAP**.

- How about **mergers** and **acquisitions**? This is a very important topic in finance that we are going to explore in this book.

- How about **company performance analysis**? We are going to evaluate company profitability metrics and ratios, such as Earnings Before Interest, Taxes, Depreciation, and Amortization (EBITDA), and more.

- We will also explore **shareholder's equity** and **dividend policy**, **risk management**, and **debt capital**, **WACC,** and project evaluation techniques like Net Present Value and Internal Rate of Return and other sources of capital available to organizations.

- We will wrap it up with a **glossary of over 100 important** terms in accounting and finance.

Let's get cracking!

Present Value Table

Periods (n)	Interest rates (r)									
	1%	2%	3%	4%	5%	6%	7%	8%	9%	10%
1	0.990	0.980	0.971	0.962	0.952	0.943	0.935	0.926	0.917	0.909
2	0.980	0.961	0.943	0.925	0.907	0.890	0.873	0.857	0.842	0.826
3	0.971	0.942	0.915	0.889	0.864	0.840	0.816	0.794	0.772	0.751
4	0.961	0.924	0.888	0.855	0.823	0.792	0.763	0.735	0.708	0.683
5	0.951	0.906	0.863	0.822	0.784	0.747	0.713	0.681	0.650	0.621
6	0.942	0.888	0.837	0.790	0.746	0705	0.666	0.630	0.596	0.564
7	0.933	0.871	0.813	0.760	0.711	0.665	0.623	0.583	0.547	0.513
8	0.923	0.853	0.789	0.731	0.677	0.627	0.582	0.540	0.502	0.467
9	0.914	0.837	0.766	0.703	0.645	0.592	0.544	0.500	0.460	0.424
10	0.905	0.820	0.744	0.676	0.614	0.558	0.508	0.463	0.422	0.386
11	0.896	0.804	0.722	0.650	0.585	0.527	0.475	0.429	0.388	0.350
12	0.887	0.788	0.701	0.625	0.557	0.497	0.444	0.397	0.356	0.319
13	0.879	0.773	0.681	0.601	0.530	0.469	0.415	0.368	0.326	0.290
14	0.870	0.758	0.661	0.577	0.505	0.442	0.388	0.340	0.299	0.263
15	0.861	0.743	0.642	0.555	0.481	0.417	0.362	0.315	0.275	0.239
16	0.853	0.728	0.623	0.534	0.458	0.394	0.339	0.292	0.252	0.218
17	0.844	0.714	0.605	0.513	0.436	0.371	0.317	0.270	0.231	0.198
18	0.836	0.700	0.587	0.494	0.416	0.350	0.296	0.250	0.212	0.180
19	0.828	0.686	0.570	0.475	0.396	0.331	0.277	0.232	0.194	0.164
20	0.820	0.673	0.554	0.456	0.377	0.312	0.258	0.215	0.178	0.149

Periods (n)	Interest rates (r)									
	11%	12%	13%	14%	15%	16%	17%	18%	19%	20%
1	0.901	0.893	0.885	0.877	0.870	0.862	0.855	0.847	0.840	0.833
2	0.812	0.797	0.783	0.769	0.756	0.743	0.731	0.718	0.706	0.694
3	0.731	0.712	0.693	0.675	0.658	0.641	0.624	0.609	0.593	0.579
4	0.659	0.636	0.613	0.592	0.572	0.552	0.534	0.516	0.499	0.482
5	0.593	0.567	0.543	0.519	0.497	0.476	0.456	0.437	0.419	0.402
6	0.535	0.507	0.480	0.456	0.432	0.410	0.390	0.370	0.352	0.335
7	0.482	0.452	0.425	0.400	0.376	0.354	0.333	0.314	0.296	0.279
8	0.434	0.404	0.376	0.351	0.327	0.305	0.285	0.266	0.249	0.233
9	0.391	0.361	0.333	0.308	0.284	0.263	0.243	0.225	0.209	0.194
10	0.352	0.322	0.295	0.270	0.247	0.227	0.208	0.191	0.176	0.162
11	0.317	0.287	0.261	0.237	0.215	0.195	0.178	0.162	0.148	0.135
12	0.286	0.257	0.231	0.208	0.187	0.168	0.152	0.137	0.124	0.112
13	0.258	0.229	0.204	0.182	0.163	0.145	0.130	0.116	0.104	0.093
14	0.232	0.205	0.181	0.160	0.141	0.125	0.111	0.099	0.088	0.078
15	0.209	0.183	0.160	0.140	0.123	0.108	0.095	0.084	0.079	0.065
16	0.188	0.163	0.141	0.123	0.107	0.093	0.081	0.071	0.062	0.054
17	0.170	0.146	0.125	0.108	0.093	0.080	0.069	0.060	0.052	0.045
18	0.153	0.130	0.111	0.095	0.081	0.069	0.059	0.051	0.044	0.038
19	0.138	0.116	0.098	0.083	0.070	0.060	0.051	0.043	0.037	0.031
20	0.124	0.104	0.087	0.073	0.061	0.051	0.043	0.037	0.031	0.026

Periods (n)	Interest rates (r)									
	1%	2%	3%	4%	5%	6%	7%	8%	9%	10%
1	0.990	0.980	0.971	0.962	0.952	0.943	0.935	0.926	0.917	0.909
2	1.970	1.942	1.913	1.886	1.859	1.833	1.808	1.783	1.759	1.736
3	2.941	2.884	2.829	2.775	2.723	2.673	2.624	2.577	2.531	2.487
4	3.902	3.808	3.717	3.630	3.546	3.465	3.387	3.312	3.240	3.170
5	4.853	4.713	4.580	4.452	4.329	4.212	4.100	3.993	3.890	3.791
6	5.795	5.601	5.417	5.242	5.076	4.917	4.767	4.623	4.486	4.355
7	6.728	6.472	6.230	6.002	5.786	5.582	5.389	5.206	5.033	4.868
8	7.652	7.325	7.020	6.733	6.463	6.210	5.971	5.747	5.535	5.335
9	8.566	8.162	7.786	7.435	7.108	6.802	6.515	6.247	5.995	5.759
10	9.471	8.983	8.530	8.111	7.722	7.360	7.024	6.710	6.418	6.145
11	10.368	9.787	9.253	8.760	8.306	7.887	7.499	7.139	6.805	6.495
12	11.255	10.575	9.954	9.385	8.863	8.384	7.943	7.536	7.161	6.814
13	12.134	11.348	10.635	9.986	9.394	8.853	8.358	7.904	7.487	7.103
14	13.004	12.106	11.296	10.563	9.899	9.295	8.745	8.244	7.786	7.367
15	13.865	12.849	11.938	11.118	10.380	9.712	9.108	8.559	8.061	7.606
16	14.718	13.578	12.561	11.652	10.838	10.106	9.447	8.851	8.313	7.824
17	15.562	14.292	13.166	12.166	11.274	10.477	9.763	9.122	8.544	8.022
18	16.398	14.992	13.754	12.659	11.690	10.828	10.059	9.372	8.756	8.201
19	17.226	15.679	14.324	13.134	12.085	11.158	10.336	9.604	8.950	8.365
20	18.046	16.351	14.878	13.590	12.462	11.470	10.594	9.818	9.129	8.514

Periods (n)	Interest rates (r)									
	11%	12%	13%	14%	15%	16%	17%	18%	19%	20%
1	0.901	0.893	0.885	0.877	0.870	0.862	0.855	0.847	0.840	0.833
2	1.713	1.690	1.668	1.647	1.626	1.605	1.585	1.566	1.547	1.528
3	2.444	2.402	2.361	2.322	2.283	2.246	2.210	2.174	2.140	2.106
4	3.102	3.037	2.974	2.914	2.855	2.798	2.743	2.690	2.639	2.589
5	3.696	3.605	3.517	3.433	3.352	3.274	3.199	3.127	3.058	2.991
6	4.231	4.111	3.998	3.889	3.784	3.685	3.589	3.498	3.410	3.326
7	4.712	4.564	4.423	4.288	4.160	4.039	3.922	3.812	3.706	3.605
8	5.146	4.968	4.799	4.639	4.487	4.344	4.207	4.078	3.954	3.837
9	5.537	5.328	5.132	4.946	4.772	4.607	4.451	4.303	4.163	4.031
10	5.889	5.650	5.426	5.216	5.019	4.833	4.659	4.494	4.339	4.192
11	6.207	5.938	5.687	5.453	5.234	5.029	4.836	4.656	4.486	4.327
12	6.492	6.194	5.918	5.660	5.421	5.197	4.988	7.793	4.611	4.439
13	6.750	6.424	6.122	5.842	5.583	5.342	5.118	4.910	4.715	4.533
14	6.982	6.628	6.302	6.002	5.724	5.468	5.229	5.008	4.802	4.611
15	7.191	6.811	6.462	6.142	5.847	5.575	5.324	5.092	4.876	4.675
16	7.379	6.974	6.604	6.265	5.954	5.668	5.405	5.162	4.938	4.730
17	7.549	7.120	6.729	6.373	6.047	5.749	5.475	5.222	4.990	4.775
18	7.702	7.250	6.840	6.467	6.128	5.818	5.534	5.273	5.033	4.812
19	7.839	7.366	6.938	6.550	6.198	5.877	5.584	5.316	5.070	4.843
20	7.963	7.469	7.025	6.623	6.259	5.929	5.628	5.353	5.101	4.870

Part 1

Questions

1 Business Types & Corporate Governance

1. Name THREE types of businesses that an individual or group of individuals can set up.
    a. A partnership
    b. A limited liability company
    c. A sole proprietorship
    d. A group proprietorship

2. What is a limited liability company?
    a. A company owned by an individual
    b. A partnership of a group of people or organizations
    c. A company that is not legally liable for its debt and liabilities
    d. A company that excludes owners from being personally liable for its debt and liabilities

3. Which ONE of the following is a benefit of a limited liability company?
    a. It cannot be sued
    b. It's not liable for its debt and liabilities
    c. The owner's private wealth and property are excluded from the company debt and liabilities
    d. The company cannot go into insolvency

4. Which ONE of the following is an example of a sole proprietorship?
    a. John and Peter just opened a shoe selling business
    b. Monica just got a loan to start her flower business
    c. John and Monica just started a limited liability company
    d. All the above
    e. None of the above

5. Which ONE of the following is not an advantage of a partnership?
   a. Easy business to establish and set up
   b. Shared financial burden
   c. Shared expertise and knowledge
   d. Owners' private wealth is excluded from the company debt and liabilities

6. Which of the following is an advantage of a sole proprietorship? Select all that apply.
   a. Easy business to set up and run
   b. Less stringent registration requirements
   c. The owner has complete control of the business
   d. Earned income is not shared
   e. All the above

7. Which ONE of the following is an example of a partnership?
   a. John and Peter just opened a shoe selling business
   b. Monica just got a loan to start her flower business
   c. John and Monica just started a limited liability company
   d. All the above

8. Which ONE of the following is an advantage of having a private limited company?
   a. Reporting requirements are less stringent
   b. The company has easy access to debt capital
   c. The company can easily buy and sell shares
   d. None of the above

9. What is the name of the system by which organizations are directed and controlled?
   a. Corporate governance
   b. Corporate direction
   c. Corporate control
   d. Corporate dependence

10. Which ONE of the following is not an advantage of listing a company on the stock exchange?
    a. Easy access to capital
    b. Improved company profile
    c. Lower listing costs
    d. All the above

11. Which ONE of the following is not a benefit of a company going public?
    a. Opportunity to raise more capital
    b. Opportunity to grow company's market share
    c. Reduced burden of complying with regulatory requirements
    d. Opportunity for individuals to sell their stake in the company

2 The Accounting Equation

12. Define the accounting equation.
    a. Assets + Liabilities = Equity
    b. Assets + Equity = Liabilities
    c. Equity + Liabilities = Assets
    d. Total Assets = Total Liabilities

13. Company B has equity of $1000 and liabilities of $500. Calculate the asset value of Company B.
    a. $1500
    b. $500
    c. $2000
    d. $2500

14. Company A has $200,000 assets and $80,000 liabilities. Calculate Company A equity?
    a. $280,000
    b. $200,000
    c. $80,000
    d. $120,000

15. Company A has an asset value of $10,000 and equity of $5000. Calculate its liabilities.
    a. $15,000
    b. $10,000
    c. $5000
    d. $20,000

16. Company A with $20,000 assets, $10,000 equity and $10,000 liabilities acquires a loan of $5000. What is the change to the accounting equation after obtaining the loan?
    a. Assets will increase by $5000; liabilities will decrease by $5000
    b. Assets will increase by $5000; liabilities will increase by $5000
    c. Assets will increase by $5000; equity will decrease by $5000
    d. Liabilities will increase by $5000; equity will decrease by $5000

17. Is a loan an asset or a liability?
    a. A loan is an asset to the borrower and liability to the lender
    b. A loan creates a liability in the books of the borrower and an asset in the books of the lender
    c. A loan is neither an asset nor a liability
    d. None of the above

18. Which ONE of the following is true?
    a. Assets will always equal liabilities
    b. Liabilities will always equal equity
    c. Assets will always equal liabilities plus equity
    d. Liabilities will always equal assets plus liabilities

19. Which of the following is not true?
    a. The difference between assets and liabilities is equity
    b. Equity is equivalent to net worth
    c. Equity is a credit balance
    d. Equity is a debit balance

20. Which ONE of the following financial statements is a perfect reflection of the accounting equation?
    a. The cash flow statement
    b. The income statement
    c. The balance sheet
    d. The bank statement

21. Company A invest $1,100,000 in a start-up. At year-end, the start-up records assets of $6,000,000 and liabilities of $3,000,000. What is the profit of the start-up?
    a. $9,000,000
    b. $10,100,000
    c. $7,900,000
    d. $1,900,000

3. The Income Statement

22. What is the other name for the profit and loss statement?
    a. The income statement
    b. The financial statement
    c. The cash flow statement
    d. The balance sheet

23. What is the cost of sales (cost of goods sold) in the income statement?
    a. All company costs including interest and taxes
    b. All company costs excluding interest and taxes
    c. Direct costs of producing goods or services sold by a company
    d. Both direct and indirect costs of producing goods or services sold by a company

24. What is sales turnover in the income statement?
    a. Total costs incurred by a company in a period
    b. Total sales generated by a company in a period
    c. Net profit
    d. Profit before tax plus net income

25. Company A records year-end sales turnover value of $4,600,000 and cost of sales value of $2,900,000. Calculate the gross profit of company A?
    a. $7,500,000
    b. $4,600,000
    c. $3,000,000
    d. $1,700,000

26. Calculate the gross profit margin of Company A (using information from question 25).
    a. 63%
    b. 61%
    c. 37%
    d. 40%

Questions 27 - 32

Company A records the following items:

Turnover $5,600,000
Cost of sales $3,900,000
Distribution costs $300,000
Administration costs $180,000
Interest charge $20,000
Other costs $50,000
Tax rate 25%

27. Calculate the gross profit for Company A.
    a. $9,500,000
    b. $1,220,000
    c. $1,700,000
    d. $1,150,000

28. Calculate the gross profit margin for Company A.
    a. 30%
    b. 35%
    c. 50%
    d. 25%

29. Calculate the operating profit for Company A.
    a. $9,500,000
    b. $1,170,000
    c. $1,700,000
    d. $1,150,000

30. Calculate the operating profit margin of Company A.
    a. 30%
    b. 50%
    c. 35%
    d. 21%

31. Calculate the profit before tax (PBT) of Company A.
    a. $1 200,000
    b. $1,220,000
    c. $1,700,000
    d. $1,150,000

32. Calculate the profit after tax (PAT) of Company A.
    a. $862,500
    b. $360
    c. $1,200,000
    d. $1,500,000

33. What is the difference between gross profit and operating profit?
    a. Gross profit is revenue minus direct costs while operating profit is revenue minus direct costs and operating expenses
    b. Gross profit is revenue minus operating expenses while operating profit is revenue minus direct costs
    c. Gross profit is revenue minus operating expenses while operating profit is revenue minus direct costs and operating expenses
    d. Gross profit is the other name for operating profit

34. Explain the difference between operating profit and profit before tax (PBT).
    a. Operating profit is profit before interest and taxes (EBIT), while profit before taxes (PBT) is profit after interest but before taxes
    b. Operating profit is revenue minus cost of goods sold (COGS), while profit before tax (PBT) is profit after interest but before taxes
    c. Operating profit is profit after taxes, while profit before tax (PBT) is profit before taxes and interest
    d. Operating profit is profit after taxes(PAT), while profit before tax (PBT)is profit after interest but before tax

35. What is the likely risk of increased borrowing on net profit?
    a. Borrowing has no impact on net profit
    b. The increased borrowing affects the balance sheet but not the income statement
    c. The increased borrowing is likely to reduce the company's net profit
    d. The increased borrowing doubles the company's net profit

36. What is the effect of an increase in tax on the profit after tax (PAT) of the company?
    a. The increased tax reduces profit after tax of the company
    b. The increased tax has zero effect on the profit after tax of the company
    c. The increased tax only affects the balance sheet
    d. The increased tax increases the company profit after tax

Questions 37 - 41

Easy Times LTD records the following items:

Revenue $4,600,700
Gross profit $2,000,000
Operating profit $1,000,000
Profit before tax $800,000
Tax $240,000

37. Calculate Easy Times cost of goods sold (direct costs).
    a. $2,600,700
    b. $6,600,700
    c. $5,500,500
    d. $6,600,500

38. Calculate the administration and distribution costs of Easy Times.
    a. $2,000,000
    b. $1,000,000
    c. $3,000,000
    d. $4,000,000

39. Calculate the finance cost of Easy Times.
    a. $400,000
    b. $600,000
    c. $200,000
    d. $300,000

40. Calculate Easy Times rate of tax.
    a. 35%
    b. 40%
    c. 25%
    d. 30%

41. Calculate the amount available to the owners of the business after paying tax.
    a. $240,000
    b. $400,000
    c. $600,000
    d. $560,000

42. Company A has experienced an increase in receivables in the balance sheet. How is this likely to impact the value of sales reported in the income statement?
    a. Reduction in the sales value
    b. No impact on sales
    c. Increase in reported sales value
    d. None of the above

43. Which of the following items is deducted from operating income to calculate net income?
    a. Rent and legal costs
    b. Administration costs
    c. Direct costs
    d. Interest and income tax

44. Which ONE of the following items is not an operating expense in the income statement?
    a. Income tax
    b. Administration cost
    c. Rent
    d. Legal costs

45. Which ONE of the following is an operating expense item?
    a. Administration costs
    b. Patents costs
    c. Cost of purchasing a building
    d. None of the above

46. What are bad debts?
    a. Money that is unlikely to be recovered from debtors
    b. The cost incurred when a customer settles a debt
    c. The cost incurred when credit is extended to a customer
    d. Money unlikely to be recovered from creditors

47. What is the difference between net profit and retained earnings?
    a. Net profit is the profit earned in the period, while retained earnings (in the balance sheet) is the accumulated net income
    b. Retained earnings is the profit earned in the period, while net profit in the balance sheet is the profit earned and accumulated from previous periods
    c. Net profit is in the balance sheet while retained earnings are in the income statement
    d. None of the above

48. What is the difference between an operating expense and a capital expense?
    a. Operating expenses are recorded in the balance sheet, while capital expenses are written off in the income statement
    b. Operating expenses are recorded as liabilities in the income statement, while capital expenses are recorded as assets
    c. Operating expenses are written off in the income statement, while capital expenditures are recorded as assets in the balance sheet
    d. Operating expenses are costs of buying long-term assets while capital expenses are costs of purchasing short-term assets

49. Company A has prepaid its building rent for July – December. The amount paid is $120K. How much will be charged to the income statement by the end of July?
    a. $120k
    b. $60k
    c. $20k
    d. $40K

4 Balance Sheet & Double Entry Accounting

50. What is an asset?
    a. Tangible resources of economic value that a company owns and controls
    b. Tangible and non-tangible resources of economic value that a company owns and controls
    c. Intangible resources of economic value that a company control
    d. Personal resources of the owners of the company

51. What is a liability?
    a. Money owed to the company by the bank
    b. Something of economic value that a person or company owes
    c. Something of economic value that a person or company owns
    d. Everything above

52. What is deferred revenue?
    a. Revenue received for goods or services provided
    b. Revenue received in advance for goods and services to be provided in the future
    c. Revenue not yet received for goods and services rendered
    d. None of the above

53. Which ONE of the following will increase the company's cash account but not the company profit?
    a. Selling a product at a loss for cash
    b. Selling a product above its cost for cash
    c. Selling a product on credit
    d. Paying off a current liability

54. Is deferred revenue an asset or liability?
    a. It's a liability
    b. It's an asset
    c. It's both an asset and a liability
    d. It's neither an asset nor a liability

55. What is deferred income tax?
    a. Income tax unpaid at the end of the accounting period
    b. Income tax paid to revenue authorities (IRS)
    c. A liability in the balance sheet due to differences in income tax recognition between the company and revenue authorities (IRS)
    d. An asset in the balance sheet due to the difference in income tax recognition between accounting standards and revenue authorities

56. What is a deferred tax asset?
    a. Money owed to the tax authorities for unpaid taxes
    b. An asset to be sold to settle unpaid taxes
    c. Money owed to the company due to overpayment of taxes
    d. Money owed to the tax authorities due to underpayment of taxes

57. Company A issues 5% loan notes at their nominal value of $50K. What is the double entry for this transaction?
    a. Debit loan notes $50K; Credit Cash $50k
    b. Debit cash $50k; Credit loan notes $50K
    c. Debit cash $50K; Credit sales $50K
    d. Debit sales $50K; Credit cash $50K

58. What is equity?
    a. Company preferred shares
    b. Company value attributable to the owners of the business
    c. Total assets and liabilities that belong to the business
    d. Total company liabilities

59. What is the other name for the balance sheet?
    a. Income statement
    b. Statement of financial position
    c. Cash flow statement
    d. Statement of shareholder's equity

60. Which ONE of the following statements best defines the balance sheet?
    a. A financial statement of the company that reports the company equity and liabilities at a specific point in time
    b. A financial statement of the company that reports its assets and liabilities at a specific point in time
    c. A financial statement of the company that reports company assets, liabilities, and shareholders' equity at a point in time
    d. A financial statement that reports company liabilities at a specific point in time

61. Which ONE of the following is a capital expense item?
    a. Administration costs
    b. Cost of purchasing a building
    c. Cost of goods sold
    d. None of the above

62. Company A obtains a loan of $500,000 to purchase a factory. What is the double entry for this loan?
    a. Debit cash $500,000; Credit liabilities $500,000
    b. Credit cash $500,000; Debit liabilities $500,000
    c. Debit building $500,000; Credit cash $500,000
    d. Debit receivables $500,000; Credit building $500,000

63. What are accounts payables?
    a. The money the company owes its suppliers
    b. The money owed to the company
    c. The money paid to the company suppliers
    d. The money sitting in the company bank account

64. What is the difference between current liabilities and long-term liabilities?
    a. Current liabilities are expected to be settled within a year, while long-term liabilities are expected to be settled after a year
    b. Long-term liabilities are expected to be settled after 5 years, while short-term liabilities are expected to be settled within 5 years
    c. Current liabilities are expected to be settled within 6 months, while long-term liabilities are expected to be settled after a year
    d. Current liabilities are similar to long-term liabilities

65. What are accounts receivables?
    a. Money owed to other companies and entities
    b. Money sitting in the company bank account
    c. Money owed to the business for goods and services sold
    d. Company liabilities and assets

66. Define current assets.
    a. Assets expected to be converted into cash after a year
    b. Assets expected to be converted into cash within a year
    c. All assets owned by a company
    d. All non-tangible assets owned by the company

67. Define non-current asset
    a. Assets that are not expected to be converted into cash within a year
    b. Assets that are expected to be converted into cash within a year
    c. All assets that belong to the company
    d. All non-tangible assets that belong to the company

68. What is the other name for non-current assets?
    a. Short-term assets
    b. Non-tangible assets
    c. Tangible assets
    d. Long-term assets

69. Which ONE of the following actions does not create a financial liability for an entity?
    a. Issue of bonds
    b. Issue of debentures
    c. Cash disposal of assets
    d. Issue of loan notes

70. Which ONE of the following actions does not create a financial asset for an entity?
    a. Buying shares in another entity
    b. Investment in bonds
    c. Issue of loan notes
    d. Investment in debentures

71. Company A purchases a car for the director for $25,000. Is this a current or non-current asset?
    a. It's a non-current asset
    b. It's a current asset
    c. It's both a current and non-current asset
    d. None of the above

72. Company A has prepaid its building rent for July – December. The amount paid is $120K. How much will be in the statement of financial position (balance sheet) as prepaid rent asset at the end of August?
    a. $120K
    b. $100K
    c. $80K
    d. $60K

73. Company A sells all its products on a cash basis. Which of the items below are you likely not to find in the financial statements of Company A?
    a. Payables account
    b. Inventory
    c. Cash
    d. Receivables account

74. What is the impact of an increase in accounts receivables and a decrease in accounts payables on the company's cash position?
    a. Increase in cash
    b. Reduction in cash
    c. No impact on the cash position
    d. None of the above

75. What is the likely impact of an increase in sales on the company's current assets in the balance sheet?
    a. Reduction in receivables and cash
    b. Increase in receivables and cash
    c. Increase in liabilities
    d. Decrease in liabilities

76. Company A purchases a building for $100,000 cash. How should this transaction be recorded in the financial statements?
    a. Credit cash $100,000; Debit non-current assets $100,000
    b. Credit cash $100,000; Debit current assets $100,000
    c. Debit cash $100,000; Credit non-current assets
    d. Credit current assets $100,000; Debit cash $100,000

77. Company A acquires a loan of $160,000 to purchase a truck. A truck is purchased for $155,000. How should this transaction be recorded in the financial statement of the company?
    a. Debit non-current assets $155,000; Debit cash $5000 and Credit liabilities $160,000
    b. Credit non-current assets $155,000; Credit cash $5000 and Debit liabilities $160,000
    c. Debit non-current assets $155,000; Credit cash $160,000 and Credit liabilities $5000
    d. Debit cash $160,000; Debit non-current assets $5000 and Credit liabilities $155,000

78. Which of the following items is not likely to be found in the balance sheet of a financial institution such as a bank or insurance company?
   a. A deferred tax asset
   b. Prepayments
   c. Cash
   d. Inventory

79. Which ONE of the following is not an asset in the balance sheet?
   a. Prepaid expenses
   b. Receivables
   c. Payables
   d. Cash

80. Which ONE of the following is not a liability in the balance sheet?
   a. Payables
   b. Long-term debt
   c. Short-term debt
   d. Receivables

81. Company A purchases materials to be used in the production of its products. Under which item should these be reported?
   a. Current assets
   b. Current liabilities
   c. Long-term assets
   d. Long-term liabilities

82. Which ONE of the following is a long-term asset?
   a. Plant and machinery
   b. Inventory
   c. Cash
   d. Prepayments

83. Which ONE of the following items is found on the balance sheet?
   a. Capital expenditure
   b. Operating expense
   c. Net income
   d. None of the above

84. Which ONE of the following is not a fixed asset?
    a. Company car used by the director
    b. Company building used in the operations
    c. Cells phones that are held for resale by a phone retailer
    d. Company machinery used in production

85. What is the difference between net assets and equity?
    a. Net assets are all company assets, while equity is the company's shares value
    b. Net assets and equity are the same things, no material difference
    c. Net assets are company tangible assets, while equity is the company's shares value
    d. Net assets are non-current assets minus liabilities, while equity is the company's shares value

86. What are tangible assets?
    a. Non-physical assets of the company such as goodwill
    b. All company's assets minus liabilities
    c. All company's physical assets
    d. Company's current assets

87. Which of the following items is not found in the statement of financial position (balance sheet)?
    a. Gross profit
    b. Payables
    c. Non-current assets
    d. Shareholder's equity

88. What is the main difference between deferred expenses and prepaid expenses?
    a. Deferred expenses are liabilities while prepaid expenses are assets
    b. Deferred expensed are assets while prepaid expenses are liabilities
    c. Prepaid expenses are current assets while deferred expenses are non-current assets
    d. There is no difference, they are both current assets

300 finance & accounting questions

89. What are intangible assets?
    a. All company's physical assets
    b. Non-physical assets such as goodwill, patents, and copyrights
    c. All company's current assets
    d. All company's assets minus liabilities

90. What are investments?
    a. Assets acquired with the intention of resale
    b. Long-term assets of a company
    c. Both long-term and short-term assets of a company
    d. Assets acquired to generate future income or appreciation

91. How should an investment in a debt instrument that will be redeemed at a premium at the redemption date be recorded in the financial statement?
    a. As a financial asset held to maturity
    b. As a financial liability held to maturity
    c. It should be written off in the income statement
    d. It should not be recorded in the financial statement

92. What is the double entry for investment income of $1,000,000 received as dividends?
    a. Debit cash $1,000,000; Credit dividends receivable $1000,000
    b. Debit dividends receivables $1,000,000; Credit cash $1,000,000
    c. Debit liabilities $1,000,000; Credit receivables $1,000,000
    d. Debit dividends receivables $1,000,000; Credit dividends receivables $1,000,000

5 The Cash Flow Statement

93. What is the difference between the income statement and cash flow statement?
   a. Cash flow evaluates the company's short-term cash position, while the income statement shows the company's profit position
   b. Cash flow evaluates the company's revenue while the income statement shows its expenses
   c. Cash flow is derived from the balance sheet while the income statement is derived from the bank statement.
   d. Cash flow evaluates the company's cash position while the income statement evaluates the company's profit position

94. Company A just purchased stock in another company. How should this activity be classified?
   a. Investing activity
   b. Financing activity
   c. Operating activity
   d. None of the above

95. Company A acquired cash through a rights issue. According to IFRS (IAS 7) under which part of the cash flow statement is this to be recorded?
   a. Under financing activities
   b. Under operating activities
   c. Under Investing activities
   d. Under investing and operating activities

96. Company A purchased a building for its expansion activities. According to IFRS (IAS 7) under which part of the cash flow statement is this to be recorded?
    a. Under financing activities
    b. Under operating activities
    c. Under investing activities
    d. Under financing and investing activities

97. Company B receives dividends from its investments, according to GAAP under which part of the cash flow statement should this be recorded?
    a. Under operating activities
    b. Under financing activities
    c. Under investing activities
    d. Under financing and operating activities

98. According to GAAP, which ONE of the following items is listed last in the cash flow statement?
    a. Financing activities
    b. Operating activities
    c. Investing activities
    d. Revenue activities

99. Which ONE of the following items is not found in the cash flow statement?
    a. Investing activities
    b. Operating activities
    c. Revenue activities
    d. Financing activities

100. What is the main difference between the direct method and indirect method of the cash flow statement?
    a. The direct method uses net income from income statement as opening balance
    b. The indirect method uses net income from the income statement as the opening balance
    c. The direct method uses accrual accounting
    d. The indirect method uses the cash accounting principle

101. Under the indirect method, adjustments must be made to the net income for non-cash transactions. Which ONE of the following items is added back to net income?
    a. Interest charge
    b. Depreciation charge
    c. Direct costs
    d. Income tax

102. How should a non-cash expense such as depreciation be treated if a direct method is used in cash flow statement preparation?
    a. It should be added back to net income
    b. It should be subtracted from income
    c. It should not be used in the calculation
    d. None of the above

103. Which ONE of the following is likely to increase the company's cash position?
    a. An increase in accounts receivables
    b. An increase in accounts payables
    c. Buying non-current assets
    d. A decrease in depreciation charge

104. Which of the following income statement items is the opening item in the cash flow statement(indirect method)?
    a. Gross profit
    b. Operating profit
    c. Revenue
    d. Net profit

105. Company A director wants to know the cash position of the company, which financial statement should she closely examine?
    a. Cash flow statement
    b. Income statement
    c. Balance sheet
    d. Statement of changes in equity

106. Which ONE of the following items is found on both the income statement and cash flow statement?
    a. Gross revenue
    b. Net income
    c. Operating income
    d. Revenue

6 Depreciation and Amortization

107. What is depreciation?
    a. A method of allocating costs of a tangible asset over its useful life
    b. A method of allocating costs of an intangible asset over its useful life
    c. A method of allocating the cost of all tangible and non-tangible over their useful life
    d. A method of allocating costs to all the non-current assets of the company

108. Should a company depreciate the land it has built factories on?
    a. Land should not be depreciated as it is a non-depreciating asset and has an unlimited life
    b. Land should be depreciated as it is a depreciating asset and has a limited life
    c. Both land and building should be depreciated because they are all non-current assets
    d. Buildings should not be depreciated but the land should be depreciated

109. Company B purchases a building for $500,000 on 1st January 2013. The building has an expected life span of 20 years and will be depreciated on a straight-line basis. Calculate the depreciation charge to be recorded in the income statement for the year ending 31st December 2013.
    a. $25,000
    b. $475,000
    c. $525,000
    d. $1,000,000

110. Should depreciation be added to the direct cost of sales (cost of goods sold)?
    a. No, depreciation is only added to the balance sheet
    b. No, depreciation is an indirect cost, so it should not be added to the direct cost of sales but to operating expenses.
    c. Yes, it should be added to the direct cost of sales because it's a direct cost
    d. Yes, it should be added to the direct cost of sales because it is an indirect cost

111. What is the impact of the depreciation charge on the company's cash position?
    a. It increases the company's cash
    b. It reduces the company's cash
    c. It doubles the company's cash
    d. It has no direct impact on the cash position

112. Which ONE of the following is not a depreciation method?
    a. Straight-line method
    b. Sum-of-the years method
    c. Declining balance method
    d. Low-balance method

113. The company purchases a car that has a useful life of 5 years. The car value is $50k. The salvage value is $5k. Calculate the depreciation charge in the first year using the sum-of-the-years method.
    a. $15k
    b. $16.7K
    c. $18K
    d. $12k

114. The company purchases a car that has a useful life of 5 years. The car value is $50k. The salvage value is $5k. Calculate the depreciation charge in the first year using the straight-line method.
    a. $9k
    b. $10k
    c. $15k
    d. $20K

115. What is amortization?
    a. The spreading of an intangible asset's cost over that asset's useful life
    b. The spreading of a tangible asset's cost over that asset's useful life
    c. Amortization is another term for depreciation
    d. Amortization is the spreading of intangible and tangible assets costs over the asset's useful life.

116. To which ONE of the following items should amortization be applied?
    a. Company loan
    b. Company machinery
    c. Current assets
    d. Current liabilities

7 Leases

117. What is a lease?
    a. A contract to purchase a non-current asset after its useful life
    b. A contract to sell a non-current asset after its useful life
    c. A contract to borrow non-current assets from another entity
    d. A contract that conveys the right to use an asset over to another entity for a specified period in exchange for a consideration

118. What is a finance lease contract?
    a. A contract that transfers control, risks, and rewards of an asset to the lessee for a specified period
    b. A contract that transfers control, risks, and rewards of an asset from lessee to lessor for a specified period
    c. A contract that does not transfer all the risks and rewards to the lessee
    d. A contract that does not transfer any risks and rewards to the lessee

119. What is an operating lease contract?
    a. A contract that allows the use of the asset but does not transfer ownership rights and control to the lessee
    b. A contract that transfers risks and rewards of an asset to the lessee for a specified period
    c. A contract that does not transfer any risks and rewards to the lessor
    d. A contract that transfers risks and rewards from lessee to lessor for a specified period

120. Who is a lessee?
    a. An entity that buys the leased asset
    b. An entity that sells the leased asset
    c. An entity to whom the asset is leased
    d. An entity that owns the asset that is leased

121. Who is a lessor?
    a. An entity that owns the asset that is leased
    b. An entity to whom the asset is leased
    c. An entity that sells the leased asset
    d. An entity that buys the leased asset

122. What is the current IFRS standard for leases?
    a. IAS 17
    b. IFRS 15
    c. IFRS 16
    d. IFRS 10

123. What is the old IFRS standard for leases?
    a. IAS 17
    b. IFRS 15
    c. IFRS 9
    d. IFRS 10

124. What is the main difference between the old IFRS standard and the current IFRS standard for leases?
    a. There is no difference between the old and new standard
    b. IFRS 16 removes the finance lease which was in the old standard
    c. There is no distinction between a finance lease and an operating lease in IFRS 16 for lessee accounting
    d. There is no distinction between a finance lease and an operating lease in IFRS 16 for lessor accounting

125. Which ONE of the following is not a feature of a valid contract containing a finance lease?
    a. The right to direct the use of the asset is identified
    b. The right to substantially obtain all the economic benefits from the use of the asset is identified
    c. The asset to be leased is identified
    d. The supplier(lessor) has the right to change the asset operating instructions

126. What is an underlying asset in a lease contract?
    a. An asset that is the subject of the lease contract between the lessor and lessee
    b. An asset that is not the subject of the lease contract between the lessor and lessee
    c. Any asset that is owned by the lessor
    d. Any asset that is owned by the lessee

127. According to IFRS 16, what is a right-of-use asset?
    a. An asset that represents the lessee's right to use an underlying asset for the duration of the lease contract
    b. An asset that represents the lessor's right to use an underlying asset for the duration of the lease contract
    c. An asset to be sold by the lessor at the end of the lease contract
    d. An asset to be sold by the lessee at the end of the lease contract

128. According to IFRS 16, what is the right-of-use asset initial measurement in the balance sheet?
    a. At fair value
    b. At value to be sold at the end of the lease
    c. At cost value
    d. At cost less depreciation

129. What is a lease liability?
   a. Amount paid at the start of the lease
   b. Lease payments outstanding at the commencement of the lease
   c. Amount to be paid at the end of the lease contract
   d. The total value of the lease contract

130. Company A acquires an asset under a 10-year lease, according to IFRS 16 what is the double entry for this transaction?
   a. Debit leases liability; Credit right-to-use asset
   b. Debit right-to-use asset; Credit lease liability
   c. Debit asset; Credit equity
   d. Debit asset; Credit current-liabilities

131. How should low-value leases (e.g., a computer) be treated in the financial statements of the lessee?
   a. They should be treated as high-value assets with right-to-use asset and liability recognized in the balance sheet
   b. They should be ignored
   c. The lease payments should be expensed in the income statement
   d. The lease payments should be treated as a liability in the balance sheet

8 Revenue

132. What is revenue?
    a. Income generated from the sale of company non-current assets
    b. Income generated from the sale of current assets
    c. Income generated from the sale of goods and services related to the company's primary operations
    d. Income generated from the sale of company shares

133. Company A cost of goods sold is $2500m and its gross profit is $3500m. Calculate the company's revenue.
    a. $1000m
    b. $4000m
    c. $6000m
    d. $6500m

134. What is the difference between revenue and net income?
    a. There is no difference between revenue and net income
    b. Revenue is earnings minus costs, while net income is profit for the period
    c. Revenue is the bottom line while net income is the top line of the income statement
    d. Revenue is the amount generated from the sale of goods and services related to the company's primary operations, while net income is revenue minus costs

135. What is the difference between revenue and net profit?
   a. Revenue is the amount generated from the sale of goods and services, while net profit is revenue minus period costs
   b. Net profit is the amount generated for the sale of goods and services, while revenue is the net profit minus total period costs
   c. There is no difference between revenue and net profit
   d. Revenue is posted into the balance sheet, while net profit is posted in the income statement

136. Which accounting standard has replaced IAS 18 and IAS 11?
   a. IFRS 10
   b. IAS 11
   c. IFRS 15
   d. IFRS 9

137. Which standard below deals with revenue from contracts with customers?
   a. IFRS 10
   b. IAS 11
   c. IFRS 15
   d. IFRS 9

9 Working Capital Management

138. What is over-trading?
    a. When a company delays paying its creditors
    b. When a company has more liabilities than assets
    c. When a company tries to engage in business activities it can barely support with its capital
    d. When a company tries to engage in business activities it can support with its capital

139. What is over-capitalization?
    a. When a company has more liabilities than assets
    b. When a company has insufficient cash flow and credit to finance its operations
    c. When a company has issued more debt and equity than its assets can support
    d. When a company has more long-term assets

140. Which of the following is a sign of over-trading? Select all that apply.
    a. A rapid increase in the current assets
    b. A rapid increase in the company's sales revenue
    c. A growing payable account
    d. A rapid increase in the company's equity capital

141. A company's trade receivable account at year-end is $500m. Its sales revenue is $2000m and its cost of sales is $800m. Calculate the company's account receivable period.
    a. 91.25 days
    b. 146 days
    c. 237.25 days
    d. 54.75 days

142. A company's trade payables at year-end are $240m, its total current assets are $700m. If the company sales revenue is $1500m and its cost of sales is $900m, calculate the company's trade-payables period.
   a. 125.14 days
   b. 97.33 days
   c. 170.33 days
   d. 58.4 days

143. A company's current ratio for the period is 1.15. Its previous period's current ratio was 0.96. What can we conclude from this information?
   a. There is an increase in liabilities and a decrease in current assets in the current period
   b. There is no change in liabilities and assets in the current period
   c. There is an increase in current assets and a decrease in current liabilities in the current period
   d. There is an increase in the company's borrowing in the current period

144. Calculate the sales revenue/net-working capital ratio for a company that has $2000m revenue, $1000m cost of sales, $900m in current assets, and $450m in current liabilities.
   a. 3.33
   b. 4.44
   c. 3.64
   d. 2.22

145. What is the significance of sales revenue/net-working capital ratio (sales to working capital ratio)?
   a. It evaluates the increase in costs relative to working capital
   b. It measures how efficiently the company is using its working capital to generate sales
   c. It measures how efficiently the company is generating working capital from the sale of capital assets
   d. It measures how well the company is decreasing its liabilities

146. Which of the following statements correctly describes the Just-in-time system?
    a. It's a system of obtaining goods from suppliers in advance of need
    b. It's a system of obtaining goods or raw materials only when they are needed to avoid holding inventory
    c. It's a system of holding high levels of inventory
    d. None of the above

147. Which ONE of the following businesses may be inappropriate to adopt the Just-in-time system?
    a. Restaurants
    b. Hospitals
    c. Phone manufacturing
    d. Construction company

148. Company A wants to minimize its inventory costs. Which of the following methods should company A adopt to minimize its costs? Select all that apply
    a. Adopting the Just-in-time (JIT) inventory system
    b. Ensuring that payables are paid early
    c. Offering huge discounts to creditors
    d. Adopting the Economic Order Quantity model (EOQ)

149. Company A has liquidity problems, which of the following actions should it take to improve its liquidity? Select all that apply.
    a. Pay its creditors on time
    b. Acquire a loan from the bank
    c. Delay paying its creditors
    d. Prompt its debtors to pay on time
    e. Delay purchase of non-current assets
    f. Suspend dividend payments.

150. Which of the following actions are appropriate for a company to take if it has surplus cash? Select all that apply
   a. Use the money to buy back its shares
   b. Suspend or reduce dividends payments
   c. Increase dividends payments account to its shareholders
   d. Make a one-off special dividend payment to its shareholders
   e. All of the above

151. Which ONE of the following is a cash management model?
   a. Baumol model
   b. Just-in-time (JIT)
   c. Regression model
   d. None of the above

152. Which ONE of the following correctly calculates the current ratio?
   a. Liabilities/Assets
   b. Current assets/current liabilities
   c. Long-term assets/Long-term liabilities
   d. Long-term-liabilities/long-term assets

153. What is the difference between the current ratio and the quick ratio?
   a. There is no difference between the current ratio and the quick ratio
   b. The current ratio is a profitability metric while the quick ratio evaluates the company's liquidity
   c. Both current and quick ratio evaluate the company's profitability
   d. The current ratio is the ratio between current assets and current liabilities, while the quick ratio is the ratio between current assets (minus inventory and pre-payments) and current liabilities

154. Company A has non-current assets of $1,500,000. Its current assets are valued at $800,000. Its long-term loan is $1,000,000 and its current liabilities are $500,000. Calculate Company A's current ratio.
    a. 1.6
    b. 4.6
    c. 1.53
    d. 1.5

10 Mergers, Acquisitions, & Reorganization

155. Which ONE of the following is not a potential benefit of an acquisition?
    a. Acquisition of assets
    b. Getting rid of a competitor
    c. Clash of cultures
    d. Access to new knowledge

156. Company A with a P/E ratio of 15 and earnings of $6m plans to buy a company B with a P/E ratio of 13 and earnings of $3.5m. The combined firm will create synergy savings of $1m and the combined P/E ratio will be 14. Calculate the maximum Company A should pay for Company B.
    a. $57m
    b. $147m
    c. $90m
    d. $46m

157. Which ONE of the following is not a type of merger?
    a. Horizontal merger
    b. Vertical merger
    c. Conglomerate merger
    d. Product merger

158. Which of the following strategies would be inappropriate to counter a hostile bid?
    a. Selling the company's valuable targeted assets without the shareholders' consent (crown jewels)
    b. Mounting a counter-bid (Pacman defense)
    c. Challenging the bid in the court of law (litigation or regulatory defense)
    d. Rights offer to shareholders to make the firm unattractive (poison pill)

159. Company A is considering a takeover bid for Company B. However, Company A does not want to suffer dilution of control after the takeover. Which of the following methods should Company A use to acquire Company B?
    a. Share for share exchange
    b. Cash bid
    c. All the above
    d. None of the above

160. Company A is considering a takeover bid for Company B. However, Company A is cash-strapped. Which one of the following methods should Company A use to acquire Company B? Select all that apply
    a. Share for share exchange
    b. Cash bid
    c. Debt for share exchange
    d. All the above
    e. None of the above

161. When it comes to mergers and acquisitions, what is an earn-out?
    a. A pricing structure where buyers must earn part of the purchase price based on the performance of the acquired business.
    b. A pricing structure where sellers must earn part of the purchase price based on the performance of the acquired business
    c. Amount paid to the directors after an acquisition
    d. The total cash amount raised during an acquisition

162. Which of the following is an advantage of expansion through mergers? Pick all that apply.
    a. A quick way to expand as the acquired business is already in operation
    b. Quick access to foreign markets through the acquired business
    c. Acquisition of company's intangible assets, such as goodwill, customer loyalty, and intellectual property
    d. High exposure to business risk if the acquired company fails to perform well

163. Which ONE of the following options is the most expensive exit strategy for a venture capitalist?
    a. Management buy-out
    b. Initial public offering (IPO)
    c. Sale to competitor
    d. Liquidate the business

164. Company A proposes a 1 to 4 share exchange for Company B. Company A has 4m shares in issue trading at $5 per share. Company B has 2m shares in issue trading at $2 per share. The acquisition will result in $3m cost savings. Calculate Company A number of shares after the acquisition.
    a. 4m
    b. 6m
    c. 4.5m
    d. 3m

165. Company A proposes a 1 to 4 share exchange for company B. Company A has 4m shares in issue trading at $5 per share. Company B has 2m shares in issue trading at $2 per share. The acquisition will result in $3m cost savings. Calculate the share price after the acquisition.
    a. $6
    b. $4
    c. $3
    d. $10

166. Company D plans on bidding for Company E. Company E has declared dividends of 30 cents per share and expects a constant growth in dividends of 5%. Company E's cost of equity is 15%. What is the value of each share in Company E?
   a. $3.15
   b. $3.00
   c. $3.30
   d. $3.20

167. If Company A buys its raw materials from Company B, which one of the following is the benefit of Company A acquiring Company B?
   a. Savings in raw material purchase costs
   b. Reduced competition from Company B
   c. Increased product range for Company B
   d. None of the above

168. Company A receives a hostile bid from Company B. Company A has large cash balances and believes that its share price is undervalued. Which method should Company A take to thwart the takeover?
   a. White knight strategy
   b. Pay a one-off special dividend (poison pill)
   c. Change articles of association to amend voting rights
   d. None of the above

169. What is a leveraged buy-out?
   a. Purchase of a private company by a group of individuals using debt
   b. Purchase of a public company by a private group of individuals using debt
   c. Buying of shares in a public listed company by venture capitalists
   d. Buying of shares in a private company by venture capitalists

170. Which ONE of the following is not an advantage of a leveraged buy-out?
    a. The company is less vulnerable to hostile takeover bids
    b. Increased management commitment due to their high stake in the company
    c. High gearing levels due to increased debt.
    d. Lower taxable income due to an increase in debt capital

171. Company Q is unlisted. Company A is considering acquiring company Q. Which one of the following is the reason for Company Q to have a lower P/E ratio than its proxy?
    a. Unlisted companies undergo less scrutiny and are less regulated
    b. Unlisted companies are always unprofitable
    c. The financial reports of unlisted companies are always full of inaccuracies
    d. None of the above

172. The company decides to sell off one of its subsidiaries. It has received offers from several external buyers but its directors are planning a management buy-out. The company decides to sell the company to its managers. Which ONE of the following is the likely reason for the company to sell to the management team?
    a. The management may have bribed someone within the board
    b. The management team has a better understanding of the company's operations
    c. The external buyers may be slow to pay for the acquisition
    d. None of the above

173. Which of the following is a disadvantage of expansion through mergers? Select all that apply.
    a. Higher premiums for the acquired company
    b. Integration problems due to different company cultures
    c. Business risk if the acquired company fails to perform well
    d. All the above
    e. None of the above

174. What is a conglomerate merger?
    a. Acquiring a company that is in a similar line of business
    b. Acquiring a company that is your major supplier
    c. Acquiring a firm that is in a completely different industry
    d. Acquiring a smaller firm

175. Which of the following constitutes a potential conflict of interest for directors in a management buy-out negotiation?
    a. Directors carrying out asset valuations of the company's assets
    b. Purchase of new company equipment by the directors
    c. Paying out new dividends
    d. None of the above

176. Which of the following is the most effective way of acquiring another company without increasing the gearing ratio? Pick all that apply.
    a. Borrow money from the bank
    b. Raising money through a rights offer
    c. Share for share exchange
    d. All the above

177. Company A intends to acquire Company B to expand into a new market. Which ONE of the following is likely to increase the wealth of shareholders of Company A?
    a. Acquiring intellectual property of Company B
    b. Firing the managers of Company B
    c. Getting rid of all employees of Company B
    d. Announcing the acquisition to the press

300 finance & accounting questions

178. Company A is considering acquiring Company B. Company A has 2m shares issued at $8 per share. Company B has $1m issued shares at $4 per share. Company A is proposing to buy Company B at $4.50 per share. A synergy of $100,000 will be created from the deal. How much wealth will be created for shareholders of Company A?
   a. $1m value created
   b. $0.3m value will be created
   c. A loss of $0.3m will be suffered
   d. A loss of 0.4m will be suffered

179. Company D is trying to acquire Company E. Company E is unlisted. The cost of equity of a listed proxy of company E is 10%. Company D is trying to use the dividend valuation model to value company E. What cost of equity should Company D use in the valuation of Company E?
   a. 10% of the proxy company
   b. The cost of equity lower than that of a proxy company, since the unlisted company has a lower risk
   c. The cost of equity higher than that of the proxy company, since the unlisted company has a higher risk
   d. Company D should use its own cost of equity

180. Company A is trying to acquire Company B. The news of the appending acquisition has pushed the share prices of both companies up. Which of the following may have caused the rise in the share prices of both companies?
   a. The market has a negative view of the acquisition
   b. The market expects the acquisition to increase the wealth of the shareholders
   c. The market expects the acquisition to decrease the wealth of the shareholders
   d. None of the above

181. What is bootstrapping when it comes to mergers and acquisitions?
    a. Increase in the value of the acquiring company's earnings per share ratio when a high-value company acquires a low-value company
    b. Increase in the value of the acquiring company's earnings per share ratio when a low-value company acquires a high-value company
    c. When a company uses borrowed money to acquire another company
    d. When a company uses a share for share exchange to acquire another company

182. What is a spin-off?
    a. Creation of a new company which is controlled by the shareholders of the original company
    b. Creation of a new company which is controlled by the shareholders of another company
    c. Creation of a new company from a failing parent company
    d. Creation of a new company from a prosperous parent company

183. Which ONE of the following is the main reason for a company to carry out a spin-off?
    a. To sell off a loss-making part of the business for cash
    b. To sell off the profit-making part of the business for cash
    c. To focus the company energies and resources on the profit-making division of the business
    d. None of the above

184. What is asset-stripping in mergers and acquisitions?
    a. When a company acquires another company with the intent of selling off its assets
    b. When a company acquires another company with the intent of using its assets
    c. Selling off part of the company to management
    d. Selling off part of the company to the public.

11 Equity and Dividend Policy

185. What are dividends?
    a. Company stock
    b. Company's net profit
    c. Company profits distributed to its shareholders
    d. Company profits distributed to its preferred shareholders only

186. Which ONE of the following is not an advantage of holding ordinary stock over preferred stock?
    a. The ordinary stock provides voting rights
    b. The ordinary stock has priority over the company's income
    c. If the company does well ordinary stock goes up in value
    d. The ordinary stockholders can elect board members

187. Which ONE of the following is not an advantage of preferred stock over ordinary stock?
    a. Preferred stock has priority access to company assets
    b. Preferred stock can be converted to ordinary stock
    c. Preferred stockholders can exercise control over corporate policy and management issues
    d. Preferred stock dividends can be paid even when the company cannot afford them

188. What is the double entry for the issuance of equity?
    a. Debit cash; Credit equity
    b. Debit equity; Credit cash
    c. Debit receivables; Credit cash
    d. Debit cash; Credit receivables

189. A company has a reported net profit of $5,000,000 and its number of shares is 10,000,000. Calculate the company's earnings per share (EPS)
   a. $0.5
   b. $5
   c. $50
   d. $0.05

190. Define dividend yield
   a. The ratio of company's number of shares to its share price
   b. The ratio of a company's earnings to its number of shares
   c. The ratio of a company's annual dividends per share to its share price
   d. Divided yield is another term for dividends paid

191. Company A is cash-strapped and is contemplating cutting down its dividends. What is the likely reaction to the news of dividend cut down? Select all that apply.
   a. The company share price is likely to fall
   b. The company share price is likely to rise
   c. Investors are likely to sell off their investment in the company
   d. All the above

192. Company A's current net profit is $500,000. It pays out a dividend of 50 cents per share. Company A share price is $5. Calculate Company A's dividend yield.
   a. 1.0%
   b. 200%
   c. 20%
   d. 10%

193. Company B's earnings per share ratio at the end of the period is 83 cents. What is Company B's dividend cover if its dividend per share ratio is 21 cents?
   a. 0.25
   b. 3.95
   c. 0.8
   d. 0.7

194. A company that is not listed has the following information:
   - $600,000 dividends paid
   - Divided growth in the foreseeable future 8%
   - Cost of equity 12%
   - Net profit $2,000,000

   Calculate the value of the company using the dividend valuation model.
   a. $5,400,000
   b. $2,000,000
   c. $3,500,000
   d. $16,200,000

195. Which of the following is a weakness of the dividend growth model? Pick all that apply.
   a. Dividend growth is erratic and rarely smooth
   b. It completely ignores capital gains
   c. It cannot evaluate companies that do not pay dividends
   d. It cannot evaluate companies with low dividends
   e. It is easy to understand and use

196. Company A has paid dividends of $500,000. Its cost of equity is 15%. Company B plans on making an offer for Company A. Calculate the value of Company A if its dividends are expected to remain the same for the foreseeable future.
   a. $3,333m
   b. $75
   c. $500m
   d. $1000m

197. A company has a book net asset value of $300m and a market value of $310m. It has 90m shares. Calculate the book value of the company per share.
    a. $2.70
    b. $3.33
    c. $3.00
    d. $3.80

198. Calculate the company's market value per share if its earnings are $20m. It has 5m $1 shares, and its P/E ratio is 6.5.
    a. $4.00
    b. $26
    c. $32.5
    d. $100

199. Company A has a P/E ratio of 18 and earnings of $36m. Calculate the company market value.
    a. $2m
    b. $54m
    c. $648m
    d. $12m

200. What do you call the invitation to shareholders to purchase additional shares in the company?
    a. Bid for shares
    b. Share purchase invitation (SPI)
    c. Rights issue
    d. Extra shares purchase

201. What is an initial public offering (IPO)?
    a. Issuing shares to institutional shareholders
    b. Repurchase of public shares by a company
    c. Repurchase of private shares by a company
    d. The initial issuance of private shares to the general public

202. Which ONE of the following is not the reason a company may pay out a higher dividend per share?
   a. Increase in company profitability
   b. Lack of investment opportunities
   c. Increase in investment opportunities
   d. To attract investors

203. Company A's market share price is $15. Its latest earnings per share ratio are 80 cents. Calculate the company's price-earnings ratio.
   a. 18.75
   b. 12
   c. 14.2
   d. 6.52

204. Which of the following is true about a company with a low P/E ratio? Select all that apply.
   a. The market perception of the company is negative
   b. The market perception of the company is positive
   c. The company's earnings yield is low
   d. The company's earnings yield is high

205. Company A has a lower P/E ratio in comparison to other companies in the same industry. Which of the following is the likely reason for the lower P/E ratio? Select all that apply.
   a. The company prospects are not positive
   b. The market expects the company to grow
   c. The company has experienced major growth in the recent past
   d. The market has low confidence in the management team of Company A
   e. The company P/E ratio is under-valued

206. Company A has 500 million $1 ordinary shares in issue. A rights issue of 1 share for every 5 held is issued. Calculate its EPS after the rights issue if profit after tax for the period is $650m.
    a. 108cents
    b. 130cents
    c. 163cents
    d. 160cents

207. Calculate Company A's theoretical-ex rights price if the company makes a 1 for 5 rights issue at $5 per share. Company A has 5m $1 shares currently trading at $6 per share.
    a. $6.15
    b. $5.83
    c. $7.0
    d. $8.23

208. Company A has 4m 1$ ordinary shares in issue. Calculate the theoretical-ex rights price if Company A makes a 1 for 4 rights issue at $6 and the current share price is $8.
    a. $5.7
    b. $5.25
    c. $7.6
    d. $5.0

209. What is the main reason for discounting a rights issue?
    a. To prevent stock price dilution
    b. To ensure the shares are attractive to shareholders
    c. To enhance stock price dilution
    d. None of the above

210. Company B with 500,000 ordinary shares of $1 each is considering raising capital through a rights issue. The current share price is $4 per share. If the rights issue is 1 for 5 shares and the issue price is $3, how much capital will be raised?
    a. $400,000
    b. $1000,000
    c. $100,000
    d. $300,000

300 finance & accounting questions

211. Which of the following is an advantage of equity finance over debt finance to an entity?
    a. Dividends are tax-deductible while interest on the debt is not
    b. Equity is cheaper than debt
    c. Dividends do not have to be paid when profits are poor
    d. Interest payments can be skipped when profits are poor

212. Company A wants to pay out a dividend of 15cents per share. It's earning per share is 90cents. Company A's current share price is $5.50 cum div. What is the Company A P/E ratio?
    a. 5.94
    b. 6.28
    c. 6.11
    d. 6.01

213. Which of the following investments provides the highest return?
    a. Ordinary shares
    b. Preference shares
    c. Corporate bonds
    d. Government bonds

214. Company A makes a bonus issue of 1 for every 4 existing shares. If the existing number of shares is 1000,000, calculate the total number of shares after the rights issue.
    a. 1000,000
    b. 1,250,000
    c. 1,200,000
    d. 1,400,000

215. Using the information from question 214, if earnings for the year are $2,500,000 calculate EPS after the rights issue.
    a. $2.5
    b. $2.0
    c. $1.5
    d. $3.0

57

216. Using information from questions 214 and 215, calculate the EPS before the rights issue if the earnings for the year remain the same.
   a. $2.5
   b. $2.0
   c. $1.5
   d. $3.0

217. Company A with 10m $1 shares and debt value of $25m has a year-end profit after tax of $5m. The whole profit is distributed to shareholders in the form of dividends. The current share price is $12. Calculate the company's cost of equity.
   a. 50%
   b. 11%
   c. 12%
   d. 4.17%

218. Company A has 2,000,000 issued shares. The current share price is $8. Calculate Company A's market capitalization.
   a. $15,000,000
   b. $16,000,000
   c. $250,000
   d. $17,000,000

219. Company B's share price is $12. Company B will pay out a dividend of $0.9 per share. Dividends are expected to grow at 4% into the foreseeable future. Calculate Company B's cost of equity
   a. 5%
   b. 6.065%
   c. 8.402%
   d. 3.074%

12 Performance Evaluation

220. Company A has a profit before tax of $10,000,000. Its tax amount is $3,000,000 and it pays $2,000,000 as dividends to its preferred stockholders. Calculate the company's return on equity if its equity is $20,000,000.
    a. 50%
    b. 30%
    c. 20%
    d. 25%

221. Which ONE of the following ratios evaluates an entity's ability to meet its short-term obligations?
    a. Earnings per share
    b. Current ratio
    c. ROCE
    d. ROE

222. Which of the following ratios does not evaluate the company's profitability?
    a. ROCE
    b. ROE
    c. Gross profit margin
    d. Quick ratio

223. Which ONE of the following is not added back to net earnings to calculate EBITDA?
    a. Amortization
    b. Depreciation
    c. Interest
    d. Direct costs

224. Which ONE of the following formulas correctly calculates EBITDA?
    a. Revenue + Interest + Depreciation + Taxes = EBITDA
    b. Revenue + Interest + Depreciation + Taxes + Amortization = EBITDA
    c. Net income + Interest + Amortization + Taxes + Depreciation = EBITDA
    d. Net Income + Interest + Amortization + Taxes − Depreciation = EBITDA

225. Which ONE of the following circumstances is more likely to make a company highlight its EBITDA performance?
    a. When it has low net income, high interest, and depreciation costs
    b. When it has high net income, low interest, depreciation, and amortization costs
    c. When it has high net income, high amortization costs, lower interest and depreciation costs
    d. When it has a lower net income, lower interest and depreciation costs

226. Which TWO of the following are solvency ratios?
    a. Return on equity
    b. A debt-to-asset ratio
    c. A debt-to-equity ratio
    d. Asset turnover ratio

227. Which ONE of the following is more likely associated with EBITDA?
    a. Liquidity
    b. Profitability
    c. EPS
    d. Dividend yield

228. Which ONE of the following reasons makes EBITDA not an appropriate measure of a company's cash flow position?
   a. It takes capital expenditure and changes in working capital into consideration
   b. It does not take capital expenditure and changes in working capital into consideration
   c. Amortization and depreciation are added back to calculate EBITDA
   d. Amortization and depreciation are not added back to calculate EBITDA

Question 229-232

Company A has the following results:

Turnover $5000m
Cost of sales $3900m
Distribution costs $300m
Administration costs $180m
Depreciation and Amortization $20m
Interest $20m
Other costs $50m
Tax rate 25%

229. Calculate Company A's net income.
   a. $1100m
   b. $620m
   c. $530m
   d. $398m

230. Calculate Company A's EBITDA.
   a. $398m
   b. $570m
   c. $530m
   d. $500m

300 finance & accounting questions

231. Calculate EBITDA to interest coverage ratio of Company A.
    a. 28.5
    b. 26.5
    c. 25.0
    d. 19.9

232. Calculate the effect on EBITDA to interest coverage ratio if the interest expenses increase to $100m.
    a. The ratio improves by 80%
    b. The ratio worsens by 80%
    c. There is no impact on the ratio
    d. The ratio improves by 70%

233. Which ONE of the following formulas calculates the return on assets correctly (ROA)?
    a. ROA = Net Income/Total Assets
    b. ROA = Net Income/Net Assets
    c. ROA = Net Income * Net Assets
    d. ROA = Net Income * Total Assets

234. Company A has a net income of $2.7b and total liabilities of $4.3b. Its shareholder's equity is $8.3b. Calculate the ROA of Company A.
    a. 62.7%
    b. 84.3%
    c. 24%
    d. 21.4%

235. What is the main difference between the Return on Equity (ROE) and Return on Assets (ROA)?
    a. ROE calculation uses equity while ROA calculation uses average assets
    b. ROE is a short-term measure while ROA is a long-term measure
    c. ROE calculation includes liabilities while ROA calculation excludes liabilities
    d. ROE is a long-term measure while ROA is a short-term measure

236. Which ONE of the following ratios evaluates how efficiently the company is using its assets to generate revenue?
   a. Return on equity
   b. Current ratio
   c. Quick ratio
   d. Asset turnover

237. Which ONE of the following is not a solvency ratio?
   a. Return on equity
   b. Interest coverage ratio
   c. Debt to asset ratio
   d. Equity ratio

238. Why would a company with poor year-end results have a high P/E ratio?
   a. A company with bad results can't have a high P/E ratio
   b. This is because the company P/E ratio is not affected by company results
   c. The market expects the company future results to improve hence the high P/E ratio
   d. The market expects the company future results to worsen, hence the high P/E ratio

239. Looking at the financial statements of Company A, the analyst concluded that the company was highly leveraged. What did the analyst mean?
   a. The company has less debt than equity
   b. The company has more debt relative to its equity
   c. The company has more assets relative to its liabilities
   d. The company is highly profitable

240. Company A has $600,000 worth of 100 par value bonds trading at $92. If its share market value is $6,000,000. Calculate the company's gearing ratio (debt/equity) using market values.
   a. 10%
   b. 13%
   c. 14%
   d. 9.2%

300 finance & accounting questions

241. Company A has a gearing ratio of 20%, its dividend yield is 12%. If the company's dividend payout ratio is 44%, calculate the company's P/E ratio.
    a. 3.67
    b. 2.39
    c. 2.99
    d. 3.41

242. Which ONE of the following actions is not likely to increase the wealth of the shareholders?
    a. Suspending dividend payout to invest in a new project
    b. A large dividend payout to the shareholders
    c. A huge borrowing to invest in a project with negative NPV
    d. A huge borrowing to invest in a project with positive NPV

243. Which ONE of the following is likely to increase the P/E ratio of a company?
    a. Poor year-end net profit
    b. Increased competition in the industry
    c. Improved prospects for the company
    d. Higher financial risks

244. Define retention ratio?
    a. The money paid to shareholders as dividends
    b. The proportion of net income retained in the business after paying out dividends.
    c. The proportion of net income paid to preferred shareholders
    d. The proportion of net income used to pay out the debt.

245. What does return on capital employed (ROCE) measure?
    a. How efficiently the company generates profit from its total capital
    b. How efficiently the company generates profit from its debt capital
    c. How efficiently the company generates profit from its short-term debt
    d. How efficiently the company generates profit from its investments

246. Company A has equity value of $2,000,000 and long-term debt of $500,000. Calculate its Return on Capital Employed (ROCE) if its EBIT is $400,000 and its net profit is $200,000.
    a. 80%
    b. 16%
    c. 20%
    d. 45%

247. Company D has Revenue of $2,000,000; Cost of sales of $1,000,000; Administration costs of $300,000; Depreciation charge of $50,000; and Interest charge of $20,000. Calculate Company D EBITDA.
    a. $700,000
    b. $650,000
    c. $630,000
    d. $600,000

13 Risk Management and Debt Capital

248. What is the difference between systematic and unsystematic risk?
    a. Systematic risk is associated with a particular industry or security while unsystematic risk is associated with the market as a whole
    b. Systematic risk is associated with the market as a whole while unsystematic risk is associated with a particular industry or security
    c. There is no difference between the two
    d. Systematic risk is a financial risk, while unsystematic risk is a business risk

249. What is the difference between business risk and financial risk?
    a. Business risk refers to the company's ability to operate profitably while financial risk refers to the company's ability to manage its debt and leverage
    b. Financial risk refers to the company's ability to operate profitably while business risk refers to the company's ability to manage its debt and leverage
    c. Financial risk and business risk is the same thing
    d. Financial risk refers to the company's ability to keep its IT infrastructure running, while business risk is about the company's ability to keep its physical assets such as buildings safe

250. Company A's shares have a beta of 1.2. The risk-free rate return is 2%. What is the cost of equity capital for Company A if its expected return to the market is 8%?
    a. 7.2%
    b. 9.2%
    c. 5.2%
    d. 10%

251. What is beta?
    a. A measure of systematic risk of a security relative to the market
    b. A measure of the unsystematic risk of a security relative to the market
    c. A measure of both systematic and unsystematic risk relative to the market
    d. A measure of company's financial risk

252. Which of the following is the reason for not having a beta for unsystematic risk?
    a. Unsystematic risk is unique to the company and can be diversified
    b. Unsystematic risk is unique to the company and cannot be diversified
    c. Unsystematic risk has the same beta as systematic risk
    d. All the above

253. Company A plans to diversify to eliminate risk. Which of the following risks can be eliminated by diversification?
    a. Market risk
    b. Systematic risk
    c. Unsystematic risk
    d. None of the above

254. Which ONE of the following is an example of risk-free security?
    a. Corporate bond
    b. Company ordinary shares
    c. Company preferential shares
    d. US treasury security

255. Which ONE of the following investments has the highest risk?
    a. Ordinary shares
    b. Government bonds
    c. Preference shares
    d. Corporate bonds

256. Which ONE of the following investments has the lowest risk?
    a. Ordinary shares
    b. Government bonds
    c. Preference shares
    d. Corporate bonds

257. Company A holds a subsidiary in another country. The subsidiary results will have to be reported in the currency of the parent company. What type of currency risk is the company exposed to?
    a. Translation risk
    b. Transition risk
    c. Transaction risk
    d. Economic risk

258. Which ONE of the following is not a type of currency risk?
    a. Transaction risk
    b. Transition risk
    c. Translation risk
    d. Economic risk

259. What is the implication of a company having a beta higher than 1?
    a. A beta of more than one (1) implies security has low volatility relative to the market
    b. A beta of more than one (1) implies security has higher volatility relative to the market
    c. A beta of more than one implies a company is profitable
    d. A beta of more than (1) implies a higher financial risk for the company

260. How does an increase in interest rates impact fixed-rate bond prices?
    a. It does not affect bond prices
    b. It reduces bond prices
    c. It increases bond prices
    d. It doubles bond prices

261. Which ONE of the following is true concerning the cost of debt?
    a. The cost of debt is lower than the cost of equity
    b. The cost of debt is higher than the cost of equity
    c. The cost of debt has no impact on the company WACC
    d. The cost of debt is equal to the cost of equity

262. Company A is highly geared while Company B is ungeared. Which one of these companies is likely to have a higher beta?
    a. Company B
    b. Company A
    c. The beta will be the same for both companies
    d. Not possible to tell with given information

263. Which TWO of the following are risks of a company holding too much cash?
    a. Hostile takeover bid
    b. Lower return on assets ratio (ROA)
    c. High liquidity
    d. Lower liquidity

264. Which ONE of the following statements is not correct?
    a. Equity is cheaper than debt
    b. High beta means security is very volatile
    c. Systematic risk cannot be eliminated
    d. Low beta means security is less volatile

265. Company A anticipates an increase in corporate tax in the coming year. Which changes to the capital structure will help counter the tax increase?
    a. Increase equity
    b. Increase debt
    c. Increase both equity and debt
    d. None of the above

266. The government is considering changing anti-monopoly laws to make it difficult for big companies to acquire small companies to eliminate competition. What risk are huge companies in this country facing?
   a. Reputation risk
   b. Fiscal risk
   c. Economic risk
   d. Regulatory risk

267. Company A is considering acquiring debt to expand its operations. What risk is Company A facing by taking on more debt?
   a. Operational risk
   b. Finance risk
   c. Business risk
   d. Fiscal risk

268. There is a risk that some of our customers will default on their debt. What risk is this?
   a. Liquidity risk
   b. Finance risk
   c. Operational risk
   d. Credit risk

269. Which ONE of the following is a positive effect of currency depreciation for a country?
   a. None, there is no positive effect for currency depreciation
   b. The country can import more products
   c. The country can export more products
   d. The country can attract more investors

270. Company A is facing legal issues for dumping toxic materials in a nearby river. What risks is the company facing?
   a. Operation and reputation risk
   b. Credit risk and finance risk
   c. Liquidity and credit risk
   d. None of the above

271. Which ONE of the following is not a derivative?
    a. Options
    b. Futures
    c. Certificate of deposit
    d. Swaps

272. It gives the buyer the right, but not the obligation to buy or sell the underlying asset, which derivative is this?
    a. Option
    b. Futures
    c. Swap
    d. Forward

273. Which ONE of the following is not a positive implication of falling interest rates for a company?
    a. An increase in consumer disposable income should positively impact demand for company products
    b. Reduced cost of borrowing (floating rate) for the company
    c. Increase in company profitability due to lower borrowing costs
    d. Reduced cost of borrowing for the company's fixed-rate loans

274. An agreement between two parties to exchange an agreed amount of a currency at a fixed rate on a fixed future date. What is the name of this contract?
    a. Currency forward contract
    b. Currency future contract
    c. Currency swap contract
    d. Currency options contract

275. Which ONE of the following is not a foreign currency derivative?
    a. Currency futures
    b. Currency options
    c. Currency swaps
    d. Currency stacks

276. Company A has 6% convertible bonds in issue. The bonds are convertible at a ratio of 10 ordinary shares per $100 nominal value bond. If the current share price is $12, what is the conversion value of a $100 nominal bond?
   a. $120
   b. $100.20
   c. $145.86
   d. $140.20

277. Company X issued some bonds a few years ago, however, due to financial difficulties Company X is struggling to pay interest on its bonds. In what category are Company X bonds likely to fall?
   a. High-yield bond
   b. Junk bond
   c. Convertible bonds
   d. Non-convertible bonds

278. Company A has 6% convertible bonds in issue. The bonds are convertible at a ratio of 10 ordinary shares per $100 nominal value bond. If the current share price is $12 and the share price is expected to grow 5% per year, what is the conversion value of each $100 nominal value bond in 4 years?
   a. $120
   b. $100.20
   c. $145.86
   d. $140.20

279. Which ONE of the following remains the same throughout the life of a fixed-rate bond?
   a. Bonds market value
   b. Bond yield
   c. Bond nominal value
   d. None of the above

280. Which TWO of the following are likely to negatively affect a company's credit rating?
    a. Defaulting on interest payments
    b. Deterioration of interest cover ratio
    c. Increase in profit after tax
    d. Increase in company free cash flow

281. Which of the following is a disadvantage of issuing a convertible bond?
    a. Share dilution and lower Earning per share (EPS) if they are converted into shares
    b. Share dilution and higher Earning per share (EPS) if they are converted into shares
    c. They do not immediately dilute the company shares
    d. None of the above.

282. Company A issues 6% loan notes at their nominal value of $100k. Calculate the company's total finance costs after 5 years when the loan is repaid at par?
    a. $30,000
    b. $25,000
    c. $15,000
    d. $10,000

283. Company A is equity and debt-financed. The ratio of equity to debt is 60:40. The cost of equity is 9% and the cost of debt is 8%. Calculate the company WACC if the tax rate is 30%.
    a. 7.64%
    b. 8.6%
    c. 8.5%
    d. 9%

284. What are convertible bonds?
    a. Bonds that cannot be sold to another entity
    b. Bonds that can be converted into equity shares
    c. Bonds that cannot be converted to equity shares
    d. Bonds that can be sold to another entity

285. Which of the following is true about non-convertible bonds? Select all that apply.
    a. They can be converted to shares
    b. They offer a lower coupon rate compared to convertible bonds
    c. They offer a higher coupon rate compared to convertible bonds
    d. They cannot be converted to shares

286. Which of the following is true about convertible bonds? Select all that apply.
    a. Bondholders are paid before ordinary shareholders
    b. Bondholders are paid after ordinary shareholders
    c. Convertible bonds cannot be converted into shares
    d. Share dilution happens when they are converted into shares

287. Which ONE of the following is not true about junk bonds?
    a. They are lower-risk bonds
    b. They are high-risk bonds
    c. They offer a high return
    d. They carry a high risk of default

288. Who are business angels?
    a. Wealthy individuals who buy out start-ups
    b. Wealthy individuals who invest in start-ups with high potential
    c. Wealthy individuals who save struggling companies
    d. Wealthy individuals who avoid paying taxes

289. Which ONE of the following is not an advantage of debt as a source of finance?
    a. Lower issue costs compared to equity
    b. Debt is tax-deductible making it cheaper than equity
    c. Interest should be paid regardless of profit position
    d. Debt can be secured against company assets making it attractive to investors

290. Which ONE of the following is not a result of converting a bond into stock for a company?
   a. A high gearing ratio
   b. Increase in the number of shares
   c. Reduction in interest payments
   d. Reduction in the number of shares

15 Investment Appraisal

291. Company A invests $200,000 in a project that will generate cash inflows of $50,000 per year. The project will last four years. The project discount rate is 7%. Calculate the project NPV.
    a. $30,650
    b. $30,000
    c. $-30,650
    d. $-30,000

292. Calculate the sensitivity to changes in a cash inflow for the project, if its initial investment is $500,000 and its cash outflow is $150,000. Its total inflows are $700,000. (All figures have been discounted)
    a. 40%
    b. 7.1%
    c. 21.4%
    d. 71%

293. Which of the following is true regarding Net Present Value (NPV)? Select all that apply.
    a. A positive NPV means that the project will not create wealth
    b. A positive NPV means that the project will create wealth for the shareholders
    c. NPV tends to favor projects that are big because they produce the biggest return for the shareholders
    d. A negative NPV means the project is not creating wealth for shareholders
    e. A negative NPV means the project is creating wealth for the shareholders

300 finance & accounting questions

294. Company A invests $9000 in a project that will last for three years. In the first year, the project expects to achieve savings of $2500. The savings are expected to rise by 7% every year because of inflation. What is the NPV of the project if the discount rate is 8%?
   a. -$2118
   b. $2118
   c. $2000
   d. $3500

295. When evaluating the viability of a project, the finance manager of Company A has been advised to use cash flows that include the effects of inflation. Which of the cash flows below should the finance manager use in the calculation?
   a. Nominal cash flows
   b. Real cash flows
   c. Positive cash flows
   d. Negative cash flows

296. Company A is undertaking a project that has three possible outcomes. If demand is high, the present value of the project is expected to be $30m; if the demand is medium, the expected present value is $20m and if the demand is low, the expected present value is $10m. There is a 0.4 probability that the demand will be high, 0.5 probability that it will be medium, and 0.1 probability that it will be low demand. What is the expected value of the project?
   a. $20m
   b. $25m
   c. $28m
   d. $23m

297. Which ONE of the following methods is not used to evaluate project profitability?
   a. Net Present Value (NPV)
   b. Internal Rate of Return (IRR)
   c. Modified Internal Rate of Return (MIRR)
   d. Return on Equity (ROE)

298. Which ONE of the following is not used to evaluate project risk and uncertainty?
   a. Sensitivity analysis
   b. Payback period
   c. Project duration
   d. Discounted payback period
   e. The discounted period

299. Which of the following is a weakness of the Internal Rate of Return (IRR)? Select all that apply.
   a. It ignores the size of the project
   b. It may not be used on projects with negative cash flows
   c. Mutually exclusive projects cannot be distinguished with IRR
   d. All the above

300. Which ONE of the following is not a weakness of the net present value (NPV) technique?
   a. It assumes that the level of risk will remain the same for the duration of the project
   b. It is not easy to find the exact discount rate that matches the project risk
   c. It is biased towards big projects, as big projects will produce a high net present value
   d. It is biased towards small projects, as small projects will produce a high net present value

Part 2
Answers

16 Answers

1. a b, c
   A partnership, a limited liability company, a sole proprietorship.
   Group proprietorship is not a type of business that can be set-up

2. d
   A company that excludes owners from being personally liable for its debt and liabilities.

3. c
   The owner's private wealth and property are excluded from the company's debt and liabilities.
   A partnership and sole proprietorship do not exclude the owners from being personally liable for business debt and liabilities.
   Owners of a partnership and sole proprietorship may have to sell personal property to settle a debt.

4. b
   Monica just got a loan to start her flower business.

5. d
   Owners 'private wealth is excluded from the company's debt and liabilities.

6. e
   All the above.

7. a
   John and Peter just opened a shoe-selling business.

8.a
  Reporting requirements are less stringent.
  A private limited company is not obligated to disclose its financial results to the public. However, a public limited company is obligated to disclose its financials to the public.

9.a
  Corporate governance.

10.c
  Lower listing costs.
  Listing a company on a stock exchange market can be a very expensive undertaking. The cost of ensuring the company complies with regulatory requirements is very high.

11.c
  Reduced burden of complying with regulatory requirements.
  Going public increases the burden on a company to comply with listing regulatory requirements.

12.c
  Equity + Liabilities = Assets
  In the balance sheet, the company's equity and liabilities are always equal to its assets.

13.a
  Assets = Equity + Liabilities
  Assets = $1000 + $500
  Assets = $1500

14.d
  Equity + Liabilities = Assets
  Equity = Assets-liabilities
        = $200,000 - $80,000
        = $120,000

15.c
Assets = equity + liabilities
Liabilities = assets − equity
= $10,000 - $5000
= $5000

16.b
Assets will increase by $5000; liabilities will increase by $5000.
A loan will increase the company's cash position (assets) and it will also create a debt (liability).

17.b
A loan creates a liability in the books of the borrower and an asset in the books of the lender.
Short-term loans will be classified as current liabilities, while long-term loans will be classified as non-current liabilities in the books of the borrower.

18.c
Assets will always equal liabilities plus equity
The golden rule of accounting is assets are always equal to company liabilities and equity.

19.d
Equity is a debit balance.
Equity is always a credit balance.

20.c
The balance sheet.
In its basic form, the balance sheet is just an accounting equation.

21.d
Change in assets = closing value − opening value
= $6,000,000 - $1,100,000
= $4,900,000
Profit = change in assets − liabilities
= $4,900,000 − 3,000,000
Profit = $1,900,000

22.a
The income statement.

23.c
Direct costs of producing goods or services sold by a company. Indirect costs are not to be included in the direct cost of sales (cost of goods sold). Indirect costs include administration costs, rent, accounting, and legal costs, and so forth. Indirect costs are also known as overhead costs. Indirect costs are not directly linked to the produced goods or services.

24.b
Total sales generated by a company in a period
Turnover is the top-line in the income statement. Net income is the bottom line.

25.d
Gross profit = sales turnover − cost of sales
= $4,600,000 - $2,900,000
Gross profit = $1,700,000

26.c
Gross profit margin = sales turnover - cost of sales
= $4,600,000 - $2,900,000
= $1,700,000
= $1,700,000/4,600,000
Gross profit margin = 37%

27.c
Gross profit = $5,600,000 - $3,900,000
= $1,700,000

28.a
Gross profit = $1,700,000/$5,600,000
= 30%

29.b
Operating profit = Turnover – the cost of sales – distribution cost – administration costs – other costs.
Operating profit = $5,600,000 - $3,900,000 - $300,000 - $180,000 - $50,000
Operating profit = $1,170,000

30.d
Operating profit margin = operating profit/turnover
$1,170,000/$5,600,000 = 21%

31.d
Profit before tax = Turnover – cost of sales – distribution cost – administration costs – other costs – interest
Profit before tax = $5,600,000 - $3,900,000 - $300,000 - $180,000 - $50,000 - $20,000
Profit before tax = $1,150,000

32.a
Profit before tax = Turnover – cost of sales – distribution cost – administration costs – other costs – interest
Profit before tax = $5,600,000 - $3,900,000 - $300,000 - $180,000 - $50,000 - $20,000
Profit before tax = $1,150,000
Tax expense = profit before tax * 25%
Tax expense = $1,150,000 * 25%
Tax expense = $287,500
Profit after tax = profit before tax – tax expense
Profit after tax = $1,150,000 - $287,500
Profit after tax = $862,500

33.a
Gross profit is revenue minus direct costs while operating profit is revenue less direct costs and operating expenses.
Once you subtract operating expenses from the gross profit you will have operating profit. Operating profit excludes interest charge/income and taxation.

34.a
Operating profit is profit before interest and taxes(EBIT), while profit before taxes (PBT) is profit after interest but before taxes. Profit before tax (PBT) is profit after financing costs/income but before the tax charge.

35.c
The increased borrowing is likely to reduce the company's net profit.
Increased borrowing may increase borrowing costs. Borrowing costs are written off in the income statement. If the company's ROA (Return on Assets) does not exceed the borrowing costs, it will negatively affect the company's net profit. The most likely effect of increased borrowing is high finance costs that will reduce the company's net profit.

36.a
The increased tax reduces profit after tax of the company. Increased taxes negatively affect the company's net income. This may negatively impact the company's investment plans.

37.a
Gross profit = revenue – cost of goods sold
$2,000,000 = $4,600,700 – cost of goods sold
Cost of goods sold = $4,600,700 - $2,000,000
Cost of goods sold = $2,600,700

38.b
Administration costs = gross profit – operating profit
= $2,000,000 -$1,000,000
Administration costs = $1,000,000

39.c
Finance cost = Operating profit – profit before tax
= $1,000,000 -$800,000
Finance cost = $200,000

40.d

Tax rate = tax charge/profit before tax
= $240,000/$800,000
Tax rate = 30%

41.d

Amount available to the owners = profit before tax – tax charge
= $800,000 - $240,000
= $560,000

42.c

Increase in reported sales value.
Receivables are linked to sales. High sales are likely to result in high receivables amounts and vice versa.

43.d

Interest and income tax.
Operating income is revenue minus operating expenses. Direct costs, administration costs, rent, and legal costs are all operating expenses. Finance and tax charge are deducted from operating income to calculate the company's net income.

44.a

Income tax.
Income tax is not an operating expense. The rest of the items are all operating expenses.

45.a

Administration costs.
Operating expenses are any day-to-day costs incurred to keep the business running. Administration costs are a good example of operating expenses. Patents and costs of purchasing a building are capital expenses.

46.a

Money that is unlikely to be recovered from debtors.
Bad debts are expensed or written off in the income statement.

47.a
Net profit is the profit earned in the period, while retained earnings (in the balance sheet) are accumulated net income.
Net profit in the income statement is profit from one period while retained earnings accumulate profit from various periods.

48.c
Operating expenses are written off in the income statement, while capital expenditures are recorded as assets in the balance sheet. Capital expenditures such as buildings are recorded in the balance sheet and depreciated through the income statement.

49.c
Pre-paid amount per month = $120K/6= $20k.
The amount consumed at the end of July is the rent amount for July. $20k will be expensed and charged to the income statement.

50.b
Tangible and non-tangible resources of economic value that a company owns and controls.
Tangible assets include machinery, inventory, and buildings. Intangible assets include patents, goodwill, trademarks, and copyrights.

51.b
Something of economic value that a person or company owes. Examples of liabilities include accounts payables, loans, and accrued expenses. Liabilities can either be current or non-current. Current liabilities are due within a year while non-current liabilities are due after one year. Examples of non-current liabilities include debentures and other long-term loans.

52.b
Revenue received in advance for goods and services to be provided in the future.

300 finance & accounting questions

53.a
    Selling a product at a loss for cash.
    Selling a product for cash will increase the company's cash position. However, it will not improve the profit position because the product has been sold at a loss.

54.a
    It's a liability.
    Deferred revenue is revenue received for goods or services not yet delivered. It creates a liability in the balance sheet.

55.c
    A liability in the balance sheet due to differences in income tax recognition between the company and revenue authorities (IRS).

56.c
    Money owed to the company due to overpayment of taxes.
    Overpayment of tax will create a deferred tax asset in the balance sheet.

57.b
    Debit cash $50k; Credit loan notes $50K

58.b
    Company value attributable to the owners of the business.
    When you subtract liabilities from assets, what remains is the company value attributed to the owners of the company. Equity is materially equivalent to net assets.

59.b
    Statement of financial position.
    According to International Financial Reporting Standards (IFRS), the balance sheet is also known as the statement of financial position.

60.c
    A financial statement of the company that reports company assets, liabilities, and shareholders' equity at a point in time.

61.b
Cost of purchasing a building.
A building is a non-current asset. A purchase of a building is a capital expense. Capital expenses are recorded as fixed assets on the balance sheet.

62.a
Debit cash $500,000; Credit liabilities $500,000
A loan increases the company's cash position, so we debit cash. It also creates an obligation to pay back the loan, so we credit liabilities

63.a
The money the company owes its suppliers.
When a company buys something on credit, an account payables entry is made in the balance sheet. Payables are current liabilities.

64.a
Current liabilities are expected to be settled within a year, while long-term liabilities are expected to be settled after a year.

65.c
Money owed to the business for goods and services sold.
When a company makes a sale or provides a service to a client on credit, a receivable account is created in the balance sheet. Receivables are assets to the business. Receivables are current assets

66.b
Assets that are expected to be converted into cash within a year.
Examples of current assets include inventory, accounts receivable, and cash equivalents.

67.a
Assets that are not expected to be converted into cash within a year.
Examples of non-current assets include land, long-term investments, company property, plant, and equipment.

68.d
> Long-term assets.
> Another term for non-current assets is fixed assets.

69.c
> Cash disposal of assets.
> Disposal of assets will not create a financial liability in the company's financial statements.

70.c
> Issue of loan notes.
> Issue of loan notes creates a financial liability for the issuing entity.

71.a
> It's a non-current asset.
> Since the company is likely to keep the asset for more than a year, this will be classified as a non-current asset or as a fixed asset.

72.c
> $80k
> Pre-paid amount per month = $120K/6= $20k
> Amount not consumed by the end of august is $20 * 4 (Sep-Dec) = $80k

73.d
> Receivable's account.
> The company will likely have no receivables account. A receivables account is usually found in the balance sheet of companies that sell on credit.

74.b
> Reduction in cash.
> An increase in receivables accounts means less cash is being collected from creditors. This may negatively affect the company's cash position. A reduction in the company's payables account implies more cash leaving the bank to settle debt, which may also negatively impact the company's cash position.

75. b

Increase in receivables and cash.
An increase in sales will result in an increase in the receivables and cash position of the company.

76. a

Credit cash $100,000, debit non-current assets $100,000.
The purchase of an asset depletes cash; hence we credit the cash account. We debit the non-current asset with the cost of the purchased asset.

77. a

Debit non-current assets $155,000; debit cash $5000 and credit liabilities $160,000.
The loan is money the business owes to the lender. The total amount of the loan will be recorded as a liability in the balance sheet. Cash will be debited with the $5000 that was not used in the purchase.

78. d

Inventory.
Banks or insurance companies are unlikely to have inventory in their financial statements. They do not sell physical products.

79. c

Payables.
Payables are a liability for the company. Prepaid expenses are recorded as an asset in the balance sheet.

80. d

Receivables.
Receivables are assets for the business.

81. a

Current assets.
The purchased raw materials are part of the inventory. Inventory is part of current assets.

82.a
   Plant and machinery.
   Plant and machinery are fixed assets or long-term assets.

83.a
   Capital expenditure.
   Capital expenditure is recorded in the statement of financial position (balance sheet) as an asset. An example of a capital expense is a building purchased by the company. A building will be depreciated through the income statement.

84.c
   Cell phones that are held for resale by a phone retailer.
   A phone retailer is in the business of selling phones, so cell phones held for resale will be its inventory, which is a current asset.

85.b
   Net assets and equity are the same things, with no material difference.
   The net asset is calculated by subtracting liabilities from assets. According to the accounting equation, equity is the difference between assets and liabilities. This makes net assets materially equivalent to equity as it represents company value attributed to the owners.

86.c
   All company's physical assets.
   Company physical assets such as property and equipment, inventory, and vehicles.

87.a
   Gross profit.
   Gross profit is not found in the balance sheet (statement of financial position). It is found in the income statement.

88. c
Prepaid expenses are current assets while deferred expenses are non-current assets.
Both prepaid expenses and deferred expenses represent costs incurred but not yet consumed. However, deferred expenses represent incurred expenses that will not be consumed within one year of the balance sheet. On the other hand, prepaid expenses are expenses that will be consumed within a year of the balance sheet.

89. b
Non-physical assets such as goodwill, patents, and copyrights.

90. d
Assets acquired to generate future income or appreciation.
Examples of such investments include shares purchased in other companies, bonds, options, and real estate investments.

91. a
As a financial asset held to maturity.

92. a
Debit cash $1,000,000; Credit dividends receivable $1,000,000

93. d
Cash flow evaluates the company's cash position while the income statement evaluates the company's profit position.
Cash flow analyzes the company's cash and cash equivalent position. The income statement evaluates the company's profit position. A company needs to understand its cash position because a profitable company that is cash strapped is bound to fail.

94. a
Investing activity.
Buying stock in another company is an investment.

95.a
> Under financing activities.
> Financing activities result in the change of the company's equity size and composition. Cash acquired through the issue of equity will be recorded under financing activities.

96.c
> Under investing activities.
> Acquisitions and disposal of long-term assets are recorded under investing activities.

97.a
> Under operating activities.
> GAAP specifies that received dividends be recorded under operating activities. However, paid dividends are to be recorded under financing activities.

98.a
> Financing activities.

99.c
> Revenue activities.

100.b
> The indirect method uses net income from the income statement as the opening balance.

101.b
> Depreciation charge.
> Depreciation is a non-cash item that must be added back to net income.

102.c
> It should not be used in the calculation.

103.b
An increase in accounts payables.
An increase in payables will imply a delay in paying creditors which will have a positive effect on the company's cash position.

104.d
Net profit
Net profit/net income is the opening line in the cash flow statement. Net income is obtained from the income statement.

105.a
Cash flow statement.
The cash flow statement evaluates how well the company manages its cash position.

106.b
Net income.
Net income is the bottom line in the income statement and it's the opening balance in a cash flow statement using the indirect method.

107.a
A method of allocating costs of a tangible asset over its useful life.
Depreciation is applied to tangible assets only. For non-tangible assets we use amortization. Depreciation is applied to long-term assets.

108.a
Land should not be depreciated as it is a non-depreciating asset and has an unlimited life.
Land is not be depreciated as it is a non-depreciating asset and has an unlimited life. However, the buildings on the land are depreciated as they have limited life.

109.a
Year-end depreciation charge = $500,000/20
= $25,000

110.b
No, depreciation is an indirect cost, so it should not be added to the direct cost of sales but to operating expenses. However, in some rare instances, a part of depreciation can be added to the direct cost of sales if part of depreciation can be directly linked to the direct costs.

111.d
It has no direct impact on the cash position.
Depreciation does not directly impact the company's cash position. However, since depreciation is usually tax-deductible, it may reduce the company's tax burden.

112.c
Declining balance method

113.a
Add the years of the useful life
Sum-of the years = 5 + 4 + 3 + 2 + 1 = 15

Subtract the salvage value from the cost of the asset

$50k - $5k = $45k

First year depreciation = 5/15 * $45K
= $15k

114.a
Subtract the salvage value from the cost of the asset

$50k - $5k = $45k

First year depreciation = $45k/5 = $9k

115.a
The spreading of an intangible asset's cost over that asset's useful life.
Amortization is for intangible assets. Depreciation is applied to tangible assets.

116.a
Company loan
Amortization is applied to non-tangible assets.

117.d
A contract that conveys the right to use an asset over to another entity for a specified period in exchange for a consideration.
At the end of the contract, the asset may either be returned to the owner, sold to the lessee, or written off, if it is at the end of its useful life.

118.a
A contract that transfers control, risks, and rewards of an asset to the lessee for a specified period.
A finance lease transfers control of the asset to the entity leasing the asset.

119.a
A contract that allows the use of the asset but does not transfer ownership rights to the lessee.
An operating lease leaves the control of the asset with the lessor.

120.c
An entity to whom the asset is leased.

121.a
An entity that owns the asset that is leased.

122.c
IFRS 16

123.a
   IFRS 16 replaced IAS 17

124.c
   There is no distinction between a finance lease and an operating lease in IFRS 16 for lessee accounting.
   For lessors accounting, IFRS 16 still allows a distinction between a finance lease and an operating lease. However, a lessee cannot classify any lease contract in their financial statement as an operating lease.

125.d
   The supplier(lessor) has the right to change the asset's operating instructions.
   If the lessor can change the asset operating instructions, then it means that control of the asset has not been transferred to the lessee. This renders the finance lease contract invalid.

126.a
   An asset that is the subject of the lease contract between the lessor and lessee.
   IFRS 16 describes an underlying asset as an asset that is the subject of a lease, for which the right to use that asset has been provided by a lessor to a lessee

127.a
   An asset that represents the lessee's right to use an underlying asset throughout the lease agreement.
   The right-of-use asset is an asset to the lessee.

128.c
> At cost value.
> The right-of-use asset is measured at cost at initial measurement. The cost value will include lease payments made at the commencement of the contract minus incentives; the present value amount of lease payments outstanding at the commencement of the contract; any direct costs incurred by the lessee. Costs that will be incurred to dismantle the asset or restore the site at the end of the lease contract will be included in the initial measurement of the right-of-use asset.

129.b
> Lease payments outstanding at the commencement of the lease.
> The present value of the outstanding payments is recorded in the financial statements as lease liability.

130.b
> Debit right-to-use asset; Credit lease liability.
> A lease contract will create an asset in the financial statements of a lessee and a liability at the same time. The asset will be depreciated according to IAS 16 over its useful life or the term of the lease (whichever is shorter).

131.c
> The lease payments should be expensed in the income statement.
> Low-value leases (usually $5000 or less) and short-term lease contracts (usually 12 months or less), the lessee is required to write off the lease payments in the income statement over the lease period. A right-to-use asset will not be created in the statement of financial position for low-value leases.

132.c

Income generated from the sale of goods or services related to the company's primary operations.

Let's say the company's primary operation is selling mobile phones, if the company sells one of its delivery vehicles, the sale proceeds will not be added to the company's revenue as it is not part of the company's primary operations, but it will be added to other income.

133.c

Revenue = cost of goods sold + gross profit
= $2500 + $3500
= $6000m

134.d

Revenue is the amount generated by the sale of goods and services related to the company's primary operations, while net income is revenue minus costs.

Income, usually denoted as net income is all earnings generated in a period less expenses. Net income is the bottom line that an entity tries to maximize.

135.a

Revenue is the amount generated by the sale of goods and services, while net profit is revenue minus period costs.

If revenue is the top line then net profit is the bottom line. Net profit is revenue less direct costs, operational costs, finance costs, and period taxes. Net profit is equivalent to net income.

136.c

IFRS 15 has replaced IAS 18 and IAS 11.

IFRS 15 replaced IAS 18 (revenue) and IAS (construction contracts). IFRS 15 is effective for periods beginning on or after 1 January 2018. IFRS 15 focuses on the transfer of control rather than the transfer of risk and rewards. Revenue is recognized once the transfer of control of an asset is established.

137.c
IFRS 15 – Revenue from contracts with customers

138.c
When a company tries to engage in business activities it can barely support with its capital.
This is when a company tries to do too much with too little. When a company engages in activities that can be barely supported by its resources then it is overtrading.

139.c
When a company has issued more debt and equity than its assets can support.
Overcapitalization will increase the interest payments that the company must make which will consequently reduce its profit and retained earnings. A reduction in retained earnings will negatively affect the prospects of the company. An overcapitalized company may ultimately go bankrupt.

140.a b and c
A rapid increase of current assets.
A rapid increase in the company's sales revenue.
A growing payable account.

141.a
Account receivable payment period = $\frac{\text{receivable} * 365}{\text{Sales revenue}}$
= $500m/$2000m * 365days
= 91.25 days

142.b
Account trade-payable period = $\frac{\text{payables} * 365}{\text{Cost of sales}}$

= $240m/$900m *365days
= 97.33days

143.c
There is an increase in current assets and a decrease in current liabilities in the current period.
An increase in current assets and a subsequent decrease in current liabilities will improve the company's current ratio. A change from a 0.96 ratio to 1.15 signifies an improvement in the current ratio of the company.

144.b
Sales revenue/net-working capital = $\frac{\text{sales revenue}}{\text{Current assets -current liabilities}}$

$$= \frac{\$2000}{\$900m - \$450m}$$
$$= 4.44$$

145.b
It measures how efficiently the company is using its working capital to generate sales
A high ratio indicates that the company is efficiently utilizing its net assets to generate sales. A low ratio indicates bad practices in working capital management, such as relying on high levels of receivables and inventory to generate sales.

146.b
It's a system of obtaining goods or raw materials only when they are needed to avoid holding inventory.

147.b
Hospitals
Hospitals are expected to hold an inventory of medical supplies. It would be risky for the hospital to adopt JIT.

148.a, d
Adopting the Just-in-time (JIT)
Adopting the Economic order quantity model (EOQ)

149. b, c, d, e, f
    Acquire a loan from the bank
    Delay paying its creditors
    Prompt its debtors to pay on time
    Delay purchase of non-current assets
    Suspend dividend payments

150. a, c and d
    Use the money to buy back its shares
    Increase dividends payments to its shareholders
    Make a once-off special dividend payment to its shareholders.

151. a
    Baumol model
    The Baumol model is a cash management model that helps a company determine how much cash to hold.

152. b
    Current assets/current liabilities

153. d
    The current ratio is the ratio between current assets and current liabilities, while the quick ratio is the ratio between current assets (minus inventory and pre-payments) and current liabilities. However, both current and quick ratios are liquidity ratios.

154. a
    Current ratio = current assets/current liabilities
    Current ratio = $800,000/$500,000
    Current ratio = 1.6

155. c
    Clash of cultures
    Clash of cultures is one of the disadvantages of acquisitions. Failure to integrate different cultures after acquisition may lead to business failure.

156.a
    First, we need to calculate the current value of company A.
    Current value of A = 15* $6m =$90m

    Second, we need to calculate the combined value of Company A and Company B.

    Combined value = new P/E *(combined earnings)
                   = 14 *($6m + $3.5m + $1m)
                    = $147m
    Now we can calculate the value of company B

    Value of company B = combined value – current value of company A
                = $147m - $90m
                = $57m

157.d
    Product merger.
    Product merger is not a type of merger.

158.a
    Selling the company's valuable targeted assets without the shareholders' consent (crown jewels).
    The crown jewels strategy would be appropriate with the approval of the shareholders. The rationale behind the crown jewels strategy is that by selling the company's most valuable assets the takeover bid will become less attractive.

159.b
    Cash bid
    A cash bid will prevent dilution of control. Dilution of control happens when there is an increase in the number of shares. With a cash bid, the number of shares will remain the same.

160.a,c
    Share for share exchange
    Debt for share exchange

161.b
A pricing structure where sellers must earn part of the purchase price based on the performance of the acquired business.
With an earn-out, the owner of the sold business obtains additional compensation only after the acquired business achieves predefined financial milestones.

162.a b, c
A quick way to expand as the acquired business is already in operation
Quick access to foreign markets through acquired business
Acquisition of company intangible assets, such as goodwill, customer loyalty, and intellectual property.

163.b
Initial public offering (IPO).
An initial public offering can be a very expensive undertaking, which makes it the least attractive exit strategy from a cost perceptive.

164.c
Number of shares before acquisitions = 4m
Acquired number of shares = ¼ * 2m = 0.5m
Company A shares = Number of shares before acquisitions + acquired number of shares
$$= 4m + 0.5m$$
$$= 4.5m$$

165.a
   Number of shares before acquisitions = 4m
   Acquired number of shares = ¼ * 2m = 0.5m
   Company A shares = Number of shares before acquisitions + acquired number of shares
   $$= 4m + 0.5m$$
   $$= 4.5m$$
   Value of new company = (Number of shares of company A * \$5) +(number of shares of Company B *\$2m) + (\$3m (cost savings))
   $$= 4m * \$5 + 2m*\$2m + \$3m$$
   $$=\$27m$$
   Share price after acquisition = \$27m/4.5m
   $$= \$6$$

166.a
   $$\text{share price} = \frac{\text{dividend}(1 + \text{growth rate})}{\text{cost of equity} - \text{growth rate}}$$
   $$= \frac{0.30 * (1 + 0.05)}{0.15 - 0.05}$$
   $$= \$3.15$$

167.a
   Savings in raw material purchase costs.
   This kind of merger is called a vertical merger. The company will have full control of the supply of raw materials needed in production. This will lead to cost savings and improved process efficiency.

168.b
   Pay a one-off special dividend (poison pill).
   Since the company has a huge cash balance, by paying a one-off dividend, the company will reduce its cash balance and make the company less attractive to takeovers.

169.b
   Purchase of a public company by a private group of individuals using debt.

170.c
   High gearing levels due to increased debt.
   High gearing levels could be the disadvantage of a leveraged buyout because it is financed through debt.

171.a
   Unlisted companies undergo less scrutiny and are less regulated.
   Since unlisted companies undergo less scrutiny compared to listed companies, unlisted companies tend to have a lower P/E ratio.

172.b
   The management team has a better understanding of the company's operations.
   The company is likely to succeed if it is sold to someone who has a good understanding of its culture and operations. The management team is in a better position to make this a success because of its proximity to the operations and culture of the company.

173.d
   All the above.

174.c
   Acquiring a firm that is in a completely different industry.
   Any merger carried out by a company that is not vertical or horizontal is a conglomerate merger.

175.a
   Directors carrying out asset valuations of the company's assets.
   Directors have vested interest, therefore them carrying out an asset valuation constitutes a conflict of interest.

176.b and c
   Raising money through a rights offer.
   Share for share exchange
   Raising money through a rights issue will not increase the company's gearing ratio. A share for share exchange can also be used to acquire another company without incurring huge borrowings that may worsen the company's gearing ratio.

177.a
Acquiring intellectual property of company B.

178.d
Current value of company B = number of shares * share price
$$= 1m * \$4m$$
$$= \$4m$$
Proposed payment by Company A = number of shares * share price
$$= 1m * \$4.50$$
$$= \$4.5m$$
Wealth created = current value of Company B + synergy − proposed payment.
$$= \$4m + 0.1m - \$4.5m$$
$$= -\$0.4m$$

179.c
Cost of equity higher than that of the proxy company, since the unlisted company has a higher risk.

Since the company is unlisted, the relative lack of marketability of its shares and the lower level of scrutiny that it is subjected to will make it riskier than the proxy, hence the need to use a higher cost of equity.

180.b
The market expects the acquisition to increase the wealth of the shareholders.

The market expectations are that acquisitions boost growth and create synergies that will benefit the shareholders.

181.a
Increase in the value of the acquiring company's earnings per share ratio when a high-value company acquires a low-value company

182.a
   Creation of a new company that is controlled by the shareholders of the original company.
   A spin-off happens when a company creates a new entity or subsidiary from its parent company. The shares of the new entity are distributed to the shareholders of the parent company.

183.c
   To focus the company energies and resources on the profit-making division of the business
   In a spin-off, a new entity is created from the old one. The new entity is owned by shareholders from the parent company. There are various reasons for spin-offs, but one of the main reasons is to focus the company's attention on the part of the business that has high growth potential.

184.a
   When a company acquires another company with the intent of selling off its assets.
   Companies usually buy an undervalued company with the intent of selling off its assets. The raised funds can be used to pay dividends for its shareholders or pay down debt.

185.c
   Company profits are distributed to its shareholders.
   The company distributes a portion of its profits to its shareholders. This profit distribution is usually once a year.

186.b
   The ordinary stock has priority over the company's income.
   Preferred stockholders have priority over the company's income. Dividends are distributed to preferred stockholders before they are distributed to ordinary shareholders.

187.c

Preferred stockholders can exercise control over corporate policy and management issues.

Preferred stockholders have no voting rights so they cannot elect directors or vote on corporate policy. They have no control over the company policy.

188.a

Debit cash; Credit equity

189.a

EPS = earnings/number of shares
 = $5,000,000/10,000,000
EPS = $0.5

190.c

The ratio of a company's annual dividends per share to its share price.
The formula for calculating dividend yield is:
Dividend yield = dividends per share/share price

191.a and c

The company share price is likely to fall
Investors are likely to sell off their investment in the company
When a company cuts its dividends, the market reacts negatively as it interprets the cut as a sign of deteriorating business conditions for the company. This is likely to result in investors selling off their shares which could cause a drop in the share price.

192.d

Dividend yield = dividend per share/ share price
Dividend yield = 50cents/500cents * 100
Dividend yield = 10%

193.b

Dividend cover = earnings per share/dividend per share
Dividend cover = 83cents/21cents
Dividend cover = 3.95

194.d
Company value = $\frac{\text{Dividends (1 * growth rate)}}{\text{Cost of equity} - \text{growth}}$
$= \frac{\$600,000 (1 + 0.08)}{0.12 - 0.08}$
$= \$16,200,000$

195.a, b and c
Dividend growth is erratic and rarely smooth.
It completely ignores capital gains.
It cannot evaluate companies that do not pay dividends.

196.a
Company value = dividends/cost of equity
$= \$500,000/0.15$
$= \$3.333m$

197.b
Net-asset value = $300m
Value per share = Net assets value/number of shares
$= \$300,000,000/90,000,000$
$= \$3.33$

198.b
Market value = P/E * Earnings
$= 6.5 * \$20$
$= \$130m$
Market value per share = market value/number of shares
$= \$130m/5m$
$= \$26$

199.c
P/E = Share price/Earnings per shares
Share market value = P/E * Earnings
$= 18 * \$36m$
$= \$648m$

200.c
> Rights issue.
> A rights issue invites existing shareholders to purchase additional shares in a company at a discount. Rights issue usually results in dilution of the stock price due to additional shares issued to the market.

201.d
> The initial issuance of private shares to the general public

202.c
> Increase in investment opportunities.
> An increase in investment opportunities will reduce the dividends distributed by the company. A company is usually encouraged to distribute its profits to the shareholders when there is a lack of investment opportunities.

203.a
> P/E = market share price/earnings per share
> P/E = $15/0.8
> P/E = 18.75

204.a, c
> The market perception of the company is negative.
> The company's earnings yield is low.
> When the market expects the company's earnings to grow it will push the stock price up which will consequently result in a high P/E ratio. When the market perception is negative it will result in a low P/E ratio. When the company's stock price is low relative to its earnings it will result in a low P/E ratio.

205.a, d and e
> The company prospects are not positive.
> The market has low confidence in the management team of Company A.
> The company P/E ratio is under-valued.

206.a
Increase in shares after the rights issue: 1/5 * 500m = 100m
Number of shares after rights issue: 500m + 100m = 600m
Earnings per share (EPS) = profit after tax/number of shares
Earnings per share = $650/600 * 100
EPS = $1.08 or 108cents

207.b
$$TERP = \frac{(N * \text{cum rights price}) + \text{Issue price}}{N + 1}$$
$$= \frac{(5m * \$6) + \$5}{5m + 1}$$
$$= \$5.83$$
*N = number of shares in issue before rights issue.
*Cum rights price = current trading price

208.c
The current market value of share capital before the rights issue:
4m * $8 = $32m
Number of issued shares after the rights issue:
¼ * 4m = 1m
Total funds raised from the rights issue:
1m *$6 = $6m
Total current market value after rights issue:
$32m + $6m = $38m
Total number of shares after the rights issue:
4m + 1m = 5m
Theoretical Ex-Rights Price = Current market value after the rights issue/Total number of shares after the rights issue.
Theoretical Ex-Rights Price =$38m/5m = $7.6

209.b
To ensure the shares are attractive to shareholders.
The rights issue is priced at a discount to the market share price to encourage the shareholders to take up the offer.

210.d
Number of issued shares = 1/5 * 500,000 = 100,000
Amount raised = 100,000 * $3
= $300,000

211.c
Dividends do not have to be paid when profits are poor.
Debt may be cheaper than equity, however, interest payments must be made when they are due regardless of the company's profit position. Dividends on the other hand are paid at management's discretion. A company may decide to hold back dividends payments when profits are poor.

212.c
P/E = Share Price/Earnings Per Share
= $5.50/0.9
= 6.11

213.a
Ordinary shares.
Ordinary shares carry the highest risk and the highest return. The potential gain from ordinary shares investment is unlimited.

214.b
Number of shares before rights issue = 1000,000 shares
Rights issue = ¼ * 1000,000 = 250,000 shares
Total number after rights issue = 1,000,000 shares + 250,000 shares
= 1,250,000 shares

215.b
Earnings per share = earnings/number of shares
= $2,500,000/1,250,000
= $2.0

216.a

Earnings per share = earnings/number of shares
= $2,500,000/1,000,000
= $2.5

217.d

Cost of equity = dividend per share/share price

First, we calculate dividends per share

Dividend per share = dividends/number of shares
= $5m/10
Dividend per share = $0.5

Cost of equity = $0.5/$12 * 100
= 4.17%

218.b

Capitalization = number of shares * share price
= 2,000,000 * $8
Capitalization = $16,000,000

219.c

cost of equity = dividends (1 + growth rate)
$\qquad$ p + g
= 0.9(1 + 0.04)
*11.1 + 0.04
= 8.402%

*P = $12 – $0.9
= $11.1

220.d

Return on equity = net income/equity
Net income is calculated from profit before tax by deducting tax amount and dividends due to preferred stockholders.
Return on equity = $10,000,000 - $3,000,000 - $2,000,000/$20,000,000
Return on equity = 25%

221.b
> Current ratio.
> The current ratio compares the company's current assets to its current liabilities. It s a liquidity ratio.

222.d
> Quick ratio.
> All the ratios except the quick ratio evaluate company profitability. The quick ratio measures the liquidity position of the company. It measures how well the company can meet its short-term obligations.

223.d
> Direct costs

224.c
> Net income + Interest + Amortization + Taxes + Depreciation = EBITDA

225.a
> When it has low net income, high interest, and depreciation costs. When a company has reported a lower net income due to high interest and depreciation costs, it is more likely that it will try to shine the spotlight on its EBITDA performance. EBITDA will be much higher than its net income

226.b, c
> A debt-to-asset ratio
> A debt-to-equity ratio

227.b
> Profitability
> EBITDA evaluates business profitability from operations before the impact of non-cash items such as depreciation and amortization and the impact of capital structure.

228.b
It does not take capital expenditure and changes in working capital into consideration.

229.d
Net income = Turnover – Cost of sales – Distribution – Administration costs – Depreciation and amortization – Other costs – Interest.
Net income = $5000m - $3900 -$300 -$180m -$20m -$50m - $20m
= $530
Net income =$530* 0.75% =397.5m

230.b
EBITDA = Turnover – Cost of sales - Distribution – Administration – Other costs
EBITDA = $5000m - $3900 - $300m - $180m - $50m
EBITDA = $570

Or

EBITDA = net income + tax + interest + depreciation and amortization
EBITDA = 398 + 133 + 20 + $20
EBITDA =570

231.a
EBITDA-to-interest ratio = EBITDA/interest cover
EBITDA-to-interest ratio = 570/20
EBITDA-to-interest ratio = 28.5

232.b
EBITDA-to-interest-ratio coverage before increase

EBITDA-to-interest ratio = EBITDA/interest cover
EBITDA-to-interest ratio = 570/20
EBITDA-to-interest ratio = 28.5

EBITDA-to-interest coverage ratio after increase to $100m

EBITDA-to-interest ratio = EBITDA/interest cover
EBITDA-to-interest ratio = 570/100
EBITDA-to-interest ratio = 5.7

Difference = 5.7 – 28.5 = -22.8
Change = -22.8/28.5 * 100 = -80%
Ratio worsens by 80%

233.a
ROA = Net Income/Total Assets.
Total assets are a combination of equity and liabilities.

234.d
ROA = net income/total assets

Let's calculate total assets value

Total assets = liabilities + equity
Total assets = $4.3 + $8.3
Total assets = $12.6

Now let's calculate ROA

ROA = $2.7/$12.6 * 100
ROA = 21.4%

235.a
> ROE calculation uses equity while ROA calculation uses average assets.
> ROA evaluates how well the company is using its assets to generate net income, while return on equity (ROE) evaluates how well the company is using its shareholder's equity to generate net income. Both ROA and ROE use net income as a numerator.

236.d
> Asset turnover
> Asset turnover is the ratio of sales revenue to average assets. It measures how efficiently the company is using its assets to generate sales revenue.

237.a
> Return on equity.
> Return on equity is a profitability ratio. It shows how well the company is using the shareholder's equity capital to generate profit.

238.c
> The market expects the company's future results to improve hence the high P/E ratio.
> The Price-Earnings ratio (P/E) is driven by market sentiments. If the market expects the company's future results to improve, it will push up the company's share price. A high share price will result in a high P/E ratio.

239.b
> The company has more debt relative to its equity.
> A highly leveraged company has more debt than equity. A highly leveraged company has a high risk of failure.

240.d
> Current market value of debt: $92/100 * $600,000 = $552,000
> Gearing ratio = $552,000/$6,000,000
>   = 9.2%

241.a
P/E = dividend pay-out ratio/dividend yield
= 44%/12%
P/E= 3.67

242.c
A huge borrowing to invest in a project with negative NPV
A negative NPV will not increase the wealth of shareholders.

243.c
Improved prospects for the company.
Improved prospects will push up the company's share price which will increase the company's P/E ratio.

244.b
The proportion of net income retained in the business after paying out dividends.
Another term for retention ratio is the plow back ratio. This is the proportion of income that is retained to be invested back in the business.

245.a
How efficiently the company generates profit from its total capital.
ROCE measures how efficiently the company is using its capital to generate profit. The formular for ROCE is:
ROCE = EBIT/Capital Employed
Capital employed = total assets – current liabilities
Simply put capital employed is shareholders equity plus long-term liabilities.

246.b
ROCE = EBIT/capital
ROCE = $400,000/$2,000,000 + $500,000
ROCE =16%

247.a
EBITDA = Revenue – Cost of Sales – Administration Cost
= $2,000,000 - $1,000,000 - $300,000
EBITDA = $700,000

248.b
> Systematic risk is associated with the market as a whole while unsystematic risk is associated with a particular industry or security.
> Systematic risk cannot be diversified, it is inherent to the market. Unsystematic risk is a diversifiable risk that is inherent to a particular stock or industry.

249.a
> Business risk refers to the company's ability to operate profitably while financial risk refers to the company's ability to manage its debt and leverage.
> Finance risk is about the company's ability to generate enough profit to meet its debt obligations. Business risk is about the company's ability to generate enough revenue to keep the business profitable.

250.b
> CAPM = risk free rate + beta (market risk − risk free rate)
> $= 2\% + 1.2(8\% - 2\%)$
> $= 9.2\%$

251.a
> The measure of systematic risk of a security relative to the market. Beta measures how a security reacts to the increase or decrease in the overall market. A beta of 1 indicates that the security moves with the market. A beta of less than 1 means that a security is less volatile than the market. A beta of more than 1 means the security is more volatile than the market.

252.a
> Unsystematic risk is unique to the company and can be diversified. Unlike systematic risk that cannot be diversified, unsystematic risk can be diversified by investing in different companies or industries.

253.c
Unsystematic risk.
Systematic or market risk cannot be diversified. It is inherent to the market.

254.d
US treasury security.
Government securities of developed countries are usually deemed risk-free. This is because the chances of the governments defaulting on the loans are almost zero.

255.a
Ordinary shares.
Ordinary shares carry the highest risk. In case of bankruptcy, ordinary shareholders will be paid last.

256.b
Government bonds.
Government bonds of rich countries are usually deemed risk-free bonds. This is because it is highly unlikely that the government will default on its debt.

257.a
Translation risk.
This is the risk that the assets, liabilities, and equity of the subsidiary will change in value when they are converted into the reporting currency of Company A. If the currency of the country in which the subsidiary is based depreciates, then the value of the assets of the subsidiary will also decline.

258.b
Transition risk.
Transition risk is not a currency risk

259.b

A beta of more than one (1) implies a security has higher volatility relative to the market.
The higher the beta the more volatile a security is relative to the market.

260.b

It reduces bond prices.
An increase in interest rate makes fixed-rate bonds less attractive to investors as the bonds will pay a lower rate. The low demand for the bonds will result in bond prices declining. The opposite happens when interest rates decline.

261.a

The cost of debt is lower than the cost of equity.
Debt is less risky than equity and interest is tax-exempt making it cheaper than equity.

262.b

Company A.
A highly geared company will likely have a higher beta because of its high finance risk.

263.a, b

Hostile takeover bid.
Lower return on assets (ROA).
A company that holds too much cash risks being a target of a hostile takeover. Too much cash also increases the number of assets relative to its profit, lowering its Return on Assets (ROA) ratio.

264.a

Equity is cheaper than debt
Debt is cheaper than equity because debt is tax-deductible. Holders of debt are paid before ordinary shareholders making debt less risky than equity.

265.b
Increase debt.
Interest is tax-deductible. Financing the company with more debt will reduce the company's tax burden to a certain extent.

266.d
Regulatory risk

267.b
Finance risk.
When a company takes on too much debt, there is a risk that it will not be able to make enough profit to cover its finance costs. The company risks defaulting on its debt.

268.d
Credit risk.

269.c
The country can export more products.
When the currency of the country is weak, it's cheaper for countries with stronger currencies to import from the country. A weak currency can boost exports.

270.a
Operation and reputation risk.
There is a risk that the legal issues will result in the suspension of company operations. There is also a risk of Company A suffering damage to their reputation due to their selfish actions.

271.c
Certificate of deposit.
A certificate of deposit is a financial product usually offered by banks.

272.a
Option

300 finance & accounting questions

273.d
Reduced cost of borrowing for the company's fixed-rate loans.
Fixed-rate borrowing is not affected by the change in interest rates.

274.a
Currency forward contract.

275.d
Currency stacks
Currency stack is not a derivative.

276.a
10 ordinary shares per $100 nominal bond
Current share price = $12
Value of $100 nominal bond = 10 shares * $12
= $120

277.b
Junk bond
Junk bonds are high-risk corporate bonds. High-risk corporate bonds have high yields

278.c
10 ordinary shares per $100 nominal bond
Current share price = $12
Share price in 4 years = $12 * 1.05^4 = $14.59
Value of $100 nominal bond = 10 shares * $14.59
= $145.9 or $145.86

279.b
Bond yield

280.a, b
   Defaulting on interest payments.
   Deterioration of interest cover ratio.
   Deterioration of the interest cover ratio indicates a drop in profit and a rise in finance costs. With falling profits, the company may struggle to pay its loans. This may negatively affect the company's credit ratings.

281.a
   Share dilution and lower Earning per share (EPS) if they are converted into shares

282.a
   $30,000
   Annual interest charge to the income statement = 6% * $100,000 = $6000.
   Since the loan is for 5 years, we multiply annual interest by 5.
   Total finance costs = $6000 * 5 = $30,000

283.a
   WACC = E/E + D * cost of equity + D/E + D * cost of debt(1-t)
   = 60/(60+40) * 9% + 40/(60+40) * 8% (1 - 0.3)
   = 7.64%

284.b
   Bonds that can be converted into equity shares.
   Holders of convertible bonds can exchange the bonds for a predetermined number of equity shares at a predetermined price at a specific date or range of dates in the future.

285.c, d
   They offer a higher coupon rate compared to convertible bonds.
   They cannot be converted to shares.

286.a, d
   Bondholders are paid before ordinary shareholders.
   Share dilution happens when they are converted into shares.

287.a
They are lower-risk bonds.
Junk bonds are high-risk bonds and offer a high return.

288.b
Wealthy individuals who invest in start-ups with high potential.

289.c
Interest should be paid regardless of profit position.
Dividends are paid at management's discretion. However, interest payments should always be paid when they are due.

290.d
Reduction in the number of shares.
When a convertible bond is converted into stock, there is an increase in the number of shares for the company. Since the company will no longer pay interest on the convertible bond, there will be a reduction in interest payments for the company.

291.c

	0	1	2	3	4
Cash flows	-$200,000	$50,000	$50,000	$50,000	$50,000
Discount rate (7%)	1	0.935	0.873	0.816	0.763
	-$200,000	$46,750	$43,650	$40,800	$38,150

NPV = -$200,000 + $46,750 + $43,650 + $40,800 + $38,150
NPV = -30,650

292.b
NPV = Project inflows − project outflows
   = $700,000 - $500,000 - $150,000
NPV = $50,000

Project sensitivity = $\dfrac{\text{NPV}}{\text{Project inflows}}$

$= \dfrac{\$50,000}{\$700,000} * 100\%$

= 7.1%

293.b, c
A positive NPV means that the project will create wealth for the shareholders.
NPV tends to favor projects that are big because they produce the biggest return for the shareholders.

294.a

	0	1	2	3
Cash flows	-$9000	$2500	$2675	$2862
Discount rate (8%)	1	0.926	0.857	0.795
	-$9000	$2315	$2292	$2275

NPV = -9000 + $2315 + $2292 + 2275
NPV = ($2118)

*savings or cash inflows will increase by 7% per year.

295.b
Real cash flows.
Real cash flows are adjusted for inflation to reflect the change in the value of money over time.

296.d
High demand = $30m * 0.4 = $12m
Medium demand = $20m * 0.5 = $10m
Low demand = $10m * 0.1 = $1m

Expected value = $12m + $10m + 1m
= $23m

297.d
Return on equity (ROE)

298.e
The discounted period.
The discounted period is not used to evaluate project risk and uncertainty.

299.d
   All the above.

300.d
   It is biased towards small projects, as small projects will produce a high net present value (NPV).

17 Glossary

Account receivable turnover ratio
- A ratio that quantifies the company's effectiveness in collecting money owed by its creditors.

Accounting equation
- The equation that represents the basic principle of accounting or bookkeeping, which state that assets should always be equal to liabilities plus owners' equity. It is also called the balance sheet equation and it is the foundation of the double-entry system.

Accounts payable
- The money the business owes its suppliers.

Accounts receivable
- The money the business is entitled to receive from customers for goods and services supplied in the past. It is an asset in the balance sheet

Accrual accounting
- An accounting method that records revenue and expenses when they occur rather than when payment is made.

Accruals
- Revenues earned or expenses incurred but not yet invoiced for.

Accrued expenses
- See accruals

Administrative expenses
- Expenses incurred in running a business that are not directly linked to the production of goods or services.

Amortization
- Method of spreading the cost of an intangible asset over its useful life

Asset turnover
- The ratio that evaluates how efficiently the company is using its assets to generate sales. It compares the sales value to the asset base.

Assets
- Tangible and non-tangible resources of economic value that the business owns or controls.

Bad debts
- Receivables that the business does not expect to collect from its customers.

Balance sheet
- Financial statements that report the company's assets, liabilities, and owner's equity at a specific point in time.

Bank statement reconciliation
- The process of reconciling the bank balance in the book of an entity to the balance reported in the bank statement.

Bond
- A loan taken out by an entity from an investor. An investor buys the bond issued by the entity.

Bond yield
- The amount of return an investor will derive from investing in a bond.

Business risk
- The possibility that a company will fail to meet its business objective of making profit.

Capital expenditures
- Expenses incurred in acquiring or maintaining fixed assets.

Capital market
- A financial market where individuals and entities buy and sell equity and long-term debt.

Capitalization
- Book value of the company's debt and equity.

Cash and cash equivalents
- Company's cash balances and investments that can be converted into cash (usually within 90 days).

Cash flow statement
- A financial statement that summarizes the cash generated and spent by the company in a specific period.

COGS
- Cost of Goods Sold

Cost of capital
- The minimum rate of return required by an investor from capital investment.

Cost of debt
- The interest that the company pays on its debt.

Cost of equity
- The return that is required by the shareholders for the capital invested.

Cost of sales
- The cost incurred to manufacture a product or provide a service. This is also known as the cost of goods sold (COGS)

Credit risk
- The risk that the borrower will default on a debt

Credit sales
- Credit sales are sales in which the amount owed will be paid in the future.

Current liabilities
- Liabilities that are expected to be settled within a year.

Debit
- An entry on the left-hand side of an account which either increases assets or decreases liabilities.

Debt to equity ratio
- A financial leverage ratio that shows the company's debt as a percentage of shareholder's equity.

Debt to total asset ratio
- A financial leverage indicator that tells how much of the company is financed by debt relative to its asset base.

Deferred expenses
- Prepaid expenses for items expected to be consumed after a year. Deferred expenses are noncurrent assets.

Deferred revenues
- Revenue received in advance for goods or services to be supplied in the future.

Depreciation
- A method of spreading the cost of a tangible asset over its useful life.

Direct cost
- A cost directly incurred in the production of an object or provision of a service.

Dividend cover
- Calculated as net income divided by the value of dividends distributed to the shareholders.

Dividend yield
- The amount of dividend paid per share expressed as a percentage of the market share price.

Dividends payable
- The amount of profit that the company has officially approved to distribute as dividends to its shareholders.

Earnings per share (EPS)
- This is profit after tax divided by the number of shares in issue.

EBITDA
- Earnings Before Interest, Taxes, Depreciation, and Amortization.

Economic order quantity (EOQ)
- The ideal quantity of inventory that a company should purchase to minimize inventory costs.

Equity
- The value of the company that is attributed to the company's shareholders.

Expenditure
- The act of spending funds by an entity.

Finance cost
- The cost of borrowing funds.

Financial risk
- The risk associated with the entity's ability to manage its debt and fulfill its financial obligations.

Financial statement
- A report that provides details of an entity's financial activities and financial position.

Fixed assets
- Long-term assets

Fixed costs
- Costs that remain the same when the level of goods or service produced changes.

GAAP
- Generally Accepted Accounting Principles

Goodwill
- An intangible asset that represents the difference between the company's purchase price and its fair value, when the purchase price is higher than the fair value.

Gross profit
- The difference between revenue and direct costs.

Gross profit margin
- Gross profit divided by revenue expressed as a percentage.

Gross sales
- Total sales reported in a period.

IFRS
- International Financial Reporting Standards.

Income statement
- A financial statement that shows the entity's income and expenditures in a period.

Income tax
- A tax imposed on income generated by an entity or an individual.

Indirect costs
- These are costs that are not directly linked to a cost object but several business activities. A good example of indirect costs is administration costs.

Intangible assets
- Non-physical assets of an entity such as goodwill.

Interest payable
- The amount of interest expense that the company has incurred but has not yet paid. It is a liability.

Interest receivable
- The amount of interest that has been earned by the company but has not yet been received. It is an asset in the balance sheet.

Internal rate of return (IRR)
- A financial metric used to evaluate the profitability of an investment.

Internal Revenue Services (IRS)
- The revenue services of the United States responsible for collecting taxes.

Just-in-time (JIT)
- A company inventory management system that only allows goods or materials to be received as close as possible to when they are needed.

Lease
- A contract that allows the lessor (asset owner) to receive regular payments from the lessee (asset user) for the use of the asset for a stipulated period.

Leaseback
- An arrangement where an entity sells an asset and leases it back.

Lessee
- The entity or person to whom the asset is leased.

Lessor
- The legal owner of the leased asset.

Limited liability company
- A company where the owners are not personally liable for the company's debt and liabilities.

Long-term liabilities
- Financial obligations of an entity that are only due after a year.

Market share
- A percentage of total sales in the market that are attributed to a particular company or product.

Matching principle
- The principle that requires a company to report expenses in the period in which the related revenues are earned.

Net book value
- The original cost of an asset minus accumulated depreciation.

Net current assets
- The difference between the total current assets minus total current liabilities.

Net income
- Net income is revenue minus all expenses and allowable deductions in a period.

Net present value
- In capital budgeting or investments, net present value is the difference between the present value of cash inflows and the present value of cash outflows.

Net working capital (NWC)
- The difference between the company's current assets and its current liabilities.

Non-current liabilities
- The company's debt that is due after a year.

Non-operating expenses
- Expenses that are not related to the company's core operations.

Non-operating income
- Income that is not derived from the company's core operations.

Operating costs
- Expenses related to the company's core operations.

Operating income
- Income that is derived from the company's core operations.

Operating lease
- A lease contract that allows the use of an asset but does not transfer the risks, rewards, and control of the underlying asset to the person or entity leasing the asset.

Operating loss
- When the company's operating expenses exceed its gross profit.

Operating profit
- Gross profit minus operating expenses. When gross profit exceeds operating expenses.

Owners' equity
- What is left when all liabilities are deducted from the assets. This belongs to the owners of the business.

Payback period
- The amount of time it takes to recoup the cost of an investment.

Period costs
- These are costs not directly linked to the manufacture of a product or the provision of a service. A good example of period costs is administration costs.

Petty cash
- The money that the business keeps to make small payments.

Preferred stock
- A class of stock that has a priority claim on the company's assets and earnings before ordinary stock.

Prepaid asset
- This is an expense that has been paid for but has not yet been consumed.

Prepaid expenses
- Expenses paid in advance. An asset in the balance sheet.

Prepaid rent
- Rent paid in advance. Reported as an asset in the financial statement.

Price-earnings ratio
- The ratio of the company's share price to the company's earnings per share.

Profit
- The difference between revenue and total expenses in a period.

Profit and loss statement
- Another name for income statement.

Quick assets
- Assets that can easily be converted into cash.

Quick ratio
- A liquidity ratio that measures the company's ability to pay its current liabilities with only those assets (excluding inventory) that can easily be converted into cash.

Ratio analysis
- The calculation of various financial ratios to evaluate the financial health of a business.

Retained earnings
- The amount of accumulated net income held by the business after dividend payments to the shareholders.

Retained earnings statement
- A statement prepared by an entity that details changes in the amount of retained earnings during a given period.

Return on Assets (ROA)
- A profitability metric that evaluates how well the company is using its assets to generate profit. Net income is divided by total assets.

Return on capital employed (ROCE)
- ROCE measures how well the company is using its capital base to generate profit. It is calculated by dividing net operating profit by capital employed.

Return on Equity (ROE)
- The ratio that evaluates how well the company is using the capital invested by shareholders to generate profit. It is calculated by dividing net income by equity capital.

Revenue
- Income generated from the sale of goods or services from normal business operations.

Rights issue
- An invitation to shareholders to purchase additional shares in the company usually at a discount to the prevailing market price.

Secured loan
- A loan backed by an asset that will be surrendered in an event of loan default.

Shareholders' funds
- The net assets of an entity.

Short-term assets
- Assets that are expected to be converted into cash within one year.

Sole proprietorship
- A business that is not incorporated and is owned by an individual.

Trade payables
- The amount of money the entity owes suppliers for goods it has received or services it has consumed.

Trade receivables
- The amount of money that an entity is legally entitled to receive from its customers for goods or services it has provided.

Treasury bills
- These are short-term debt obligations issued by the government with a maturity of a year or less.

Trial balance
- This is a list of closing ledger balances of all ledger accounts in the general ledger compiled into debit and credit columns. The sum of the debit columns must always equal the sum of the credit columns.

Turnover
- Total sales made by the business in a period.

Unsecured loan
- A loan that is not backed by collateral. It is not tied up to any asset.

US treasury bonds
- These are debt securities issued by the United States government with a maturity of at least 20 years.

Variable cost
- The type of cost that changes when the level of production changes.

WACC
- Weighted Average Cost of Capital.

Withholding tax
- Tax paid by the individual or entity that is paying income rather than the entity or individual receiving income.

Working capital
- The difference between the company's current assets and current liabilities. This is the amount available to the company for its day-to-day operations.

Working capital ratio
- The ratio measures the company's liquidity. It is calculated by dividing current assets by current liabilities.

Zero-coupon bond
- A bond that does not pay interest, is issued at a discount and redeemed at par.

Your Notes

About Author

The author is a chartered accountant (CA) (CIMA & ACCA) who is committed to helping others learn about accounting and finance.

You can reach him at: benjaminbennettalexander@gmail.com

Website: http://www.financequestionsworld.com

300 finance & accounting questions

www.ingramcontent.com/pod-product-compliance
Lightning Source LLC
Chambersburg PA
CBHW081429220526
45466CB00008B/2325